STUDIES

This series, p   Sociological
Association,   ensive and
scholarly tr   The books
do not off   the current   research in
various fi   matter   ch are the
subject of   to cover a
broad ran   1) abstract
problems   interpretative
questions   s: (3) issues
in empiri   slations
of import   ly been
available   ibution
to its par   ader an
indication   notated
bibliogra   further
literature   GIDDENS

University   ambridge

STUDIES IN SOCIOLOGY

General Editor: ANTHONY GIDDENS

Editorial Advisers: T. B. BOTTOMORE, DAVID LOCKWOOD and ERNEST GELLNER

Published

THE SOCIOLOGY OF SOCIAL MOVEMENTS
J. A. Banks

KNOWLEDGE AND IDEOLOGY IN THE SOCIOLOGY OF EDUCATION
Gerald Bernbaum

MARXIST SOCIOLOGY
Tom Bottomore

POLITICS AND SOCIOLOGY IN THE THOUGHT OF MAX WEBER
Anthony Giddens

THE USE OF OFFICIAL STATISTICS IN SOCIOLOGY
Barry Hindess

STRIKES AND INDUSTRIAL CONFLICT: BRITAIN AND SCANDINAVIA
Geoffrey K. Ingham

PROFESSIONS AND POWER
Terence J. Johnson

POWER: A RADICAL VIEW
Steven Lukes

THE ORGANISATION OF CRIME
Mary McIntosh

CONSCIOUSNESS AND ACTION AMONG THE WESTERN WORKING CLASS
Michael Mann

THE SOCIAL PROCESS OF INNOVATION: A STUDY IN THE SOCIOLOGY OF SCIENCE
M. J. Mulkay

Forthcoming

THE DEVELOPMENT OF THE SOCIOLOGY OF KNOWLEDGE
Steven Lukes

CLASS THEORY AND THE DIVISION OF LABOUR
Gavin Mackenzie

Marxist Sociology

TOM BOTTOMORE

Professor of Sociology, University of Sussex

First edition 1975
Reprinted 1979

Published by
THE MACMILLAN PRESS LTD
London and Basingstoke
Associated companies in Delhi Dublin
Hong Kong Johannesburg Lagos Melbourne
New York Singapore and Tokyo

ISBN 0 333 13774 4

Printed in Great Britain by
THE ANCHOR PRESS LTD
Tiptree, Essex

CONTENTS

1. INTRODUCTION

The debate about a Marxist sociology has gone on for a long time. Indeed, it may be said to have begun with Marx himself, not in his occasional slighting references to Comte, but in those passages – unfortunately all too few – in which he reflected upon the aims and methods of his own studies.

Marx's criticisms of Comte, and still more of his disciples in France and England, were not directed against Comte's intention to construct a general social science and to formulate historical laws (that is, against his 'positivism'),[1] but against the form which this new science took, and against the political doctrines which were derived from it. Comte's synthesis, Marx considered, was 'miserable compared to Hegel'.[2] The comparison itself is instructive, for one major element in Comte's theory to which Marx would have been particularly unsympathetic is the 'law of the three stages', which interprets historical change in terms of the development of mind, and in this respect resembles Hegel's philosophy of history. On another occasion, referring to the ideas of

[1] I shall use the term 'positivism' throughout this study in a very broad sense to characterise an approach to the social sciences which regards them as being essentially the same as the natural sciences, aiming at the formulation of general causal laws, resting their claims to valid knowledge upon the analysis of some empirical reality, not upon philosophical intuition, and thus asserting the unity of scientific method; and which makes a sharp distinction between scientific statements and value judgements. Comte's doctrine is only one particular version of positivism. There are useful general accounts of positivism in D. G. Charlton, *Positivist Thought in France during the Second Empire, 1852–1870* (Oxford : Clarendon Press, 1959) and Leszek Kolakowski, *Positivist Philosophy* (Harmondsworth : Penguin, 1972).

[2] Marx to Engels, 7 July 1866.

an English Positivist, E. S. Beesly, Marx commented that 'positivism equals ignorance of everything positive',[1] and this too must
be read as a criticism of the tendency among the Comtean Positivists to emphasise the moral and intellectual factors, rather than
economic changes and class relations, in social development.

Marx, it is clear, considered that his own social theory was
closer to being a positive science than was Comte's Positivism, and
this element in his thought was strongly established long before
he read Comte. In fact, it was derived in part from the same
source as Comte's own views, namely from the writings of Saint-
Simon, and it was nourished further by the outline of a new social
science presented by Lorenz von Stein in the first edition (1842)
of his study of the French socialist thinkers, *The Social Movement in France*.

But there was another strand in Marx's thought, which came
from his reading of Kant, Fichte and Hegel. In this framework
of ideas the main problem was not that of elaborating a science
which would provide a rigorous causal account of social events,
but of overcoming the separation between 'is' and 'ought', which
Kant had established and positivism had reasserted, in order to
construct a theory of ethics and politics and thus make possible
a practical intervention in the course of social life based upon
something more than subjective caprice. Marx wrestled with this
question, of how to find the 'Idea in the real world itself',[2] until he
reached the crucial turning-point in his thought with his discovery of the 'proletariat', which was at the same time a *necessary*
product of modern capitalist society and the embodiment or
representative in the real world of a new moral and political ideal.

In this conception of the proletariat as a revolutionary class,

[1] Marx to Engels, 20 March 1869. On some political issues Marx
was quite close to Beesly, but this can be explained, in part, by the
fact that Beesly did diverge from the views of other positivists and
could be treated by Marx as some kind of 'incipient Marxist'. See
the study by Royden Harrison, 'E. S. Beesly and Karl Marx',
International Review of Social History, iv, parts 1 and 2 (1959)
22–58, 208–38; especially 230–7.

[2] See his letter to his father, 10 November 1837, translated in
Loyd D. Easton and Kurt H. Guddat (eds), *Writings of the Young
Marx on Philosophy and Society* (Garden City, N.Y.: Doubleday
Anchor, 1967) pp. 40–50.

and more generally in his view of the role of social classes in the historical development of society, Marx was able to bring together the two strands of his thought – positivist and Hegelian – but it is by no means clear that they were integrated in a superior methodological conception of the nature of a general social science, rather than juxtaposed in a specific historical context which obscured the problem of the tension between explanation and valuation. Marx never wrote an exposition of his methodology in the style of Durkheim's *Rules of Sociological Method* or Max Weber's long essay on 'Objectivity in Social Science and Social Policy'; nor did his work receive any widespread critical attention during his lifetime, such as would have led him to defend his theory in a systematic way. As Croce once observed, '. . . the doctrine of historical materialism is not embodied in a classical and definitive book . . .'. Hence, Marx's methodological views, in relation to the two lines of thought I have distinguished, must be reconstructed from fragmentary and dispersed comments, and this has permitted a considerable diversity of subsequent interpretation.

In the present study I shall not be concerned directly with Marx's own methodology,[1] but mainly with the interpretations of later Marxist writers which led them to expound particular sociological theses, to criticise other sociological theories, or to question, in a more general way, the position of sociology as a science of society. For this purpose it is only necessary to establish, as a starting-point, that Marx's conceptions were capable of giving rise, in one direction, to a broadly positivist sociology, and in another direction to a style of thought which has generally been referred to as 'critical philosophy'; and that these possibilities existed side by side in his thought from the outset, even though the emphasis in his early writings appears more Hegelian, and in his later writings more positivist.[2]

[1] I hope to publish shortly a general critique of Marx's methodological views, in which I shall examine more fully than I can do here the relation of Marx's thought to positivism, to empiricism, and to the whole question of a 'natural science' of society.

[2] Hence it can be argued, though I think mistakenly, that 'the particular contribution of Marx was to transform this notion [an activist concept of *praxis* developed by the Young Hegelians] into a theory of action from which in later years there emerged a deter-

Merely to illustrate this difference we can contrast Marx's statements in the *Theses on Feuerbach* about Feuerbach's failure to 'grasp the significance of "revolutionary", "practical–critical" activity', about the rational understanding of 'the coincidence of the changing circumstances and of human activity or self-changing' as revolutionary practice, and about the need to change the world as well as, or instead of, *interpreting* it, with his approving citation in the preface to the second German edition of *Capital*, vol. 1, from one of the few serious reviews of his work: 'Marx regards the social movement as a natural sequence of historical phenomena, governed by laws which are not only independent of the will, the consciousness, and the purposes of men, but on the contrary, determine their volition, consciousness and purposes.' On this Marx commented that the reviewer '. . . describes so aptly . . . the method I have actually used . . . the dialectical method'.

But then we should have to note that in his early writings Marx already formulated the idea of a positive science of society when he wrote in the *Economic and Philosophical Manuscripts* (1844) that 'natural science will one day incorporate the science of man, just as the science of man will incorporate natural science; there will be a *single* science', or that 'the natural sciences . . . will become the basis of a human science'; and in *The German Ideology* (1845) that 'where speculation ends – in real life – there real positive science begins: the representation of the practical process of development of men'. On the other side, there is still to be found in Marx's later writings – in spite of the apparent predominance of a deterministic sociology – the assertion of man's freedom and creativity and thus of his ability to intervene consciously and deliberately to change the course of social life; for

---

minist sociology'; George Lichtheim, *From Marx to Hegel* (London: Orbach & Chambers, 1971) p. 14. Other commentators, however, have taken a view closer to that which I expound here, according to which the idea of a scientific sociology was always present in Marx's thought; see, for example, Albrecht Wellmer's discussion of Marx's 'latent positivism', in his book *Critical Theory of Society* (New York: Herder & Herder, 1971). I shall examine later the type of argument that Wellmer and other exponents of 'critical theory' develop.

example, in many passages of the *Grundrisse* (1857–8) on the development of a richer, more complex human individual in modern society, who has then to struggle against the limitations imposed by the capitalist social system, or in the preface to the *Enquête ouvrière* (1880) in which the industrial workers are urged to take action to 'remedy the social ills from which they suffer'.

The working out of these two themes – science and revolution – constitutes the history of Marxist thought during the past century. The development of this thought has taken place in the midst of profound economic and political changes, and in an intellectual environment greatly affected by the luxuriant growth of the social sciences. But I shall not be concerned here to examine in any detail this wider context, to set forth a history of ideas or a sociological interpretation of Marxist thought.[1] My aim will be, first, to elucidate the theoretical foundations of the attempts to constitute Marxism as a system of sociology, and secondly, to assess the criticisms which have been brought against such endeavours from the perspective of those thinkers who see Marxism as a philosophical world view or a critical philosophy of history – criticisms which broaden out into arguments against the possibility or desirability of any positivist social science. These controversies have turned, to a large extent, upon the issue of the relation between social theory and social practice, and the characteristic features of the opposing views can be more sharply delineated through an analysis of this question, which has, in any case, become once more the centre of wide-ranging methodological disputes among sociologists. Finally, I shall consider how far, and in what manner, the analysis of the institutional framework and the main tendencies of development, in modern societies, has been advanced, or can now be advanced, by the use of Marxist concepts, or of what is loosely called a 'Marxist method'.

[1] For studies along these lines the reader should consult H. Stuart Hughes, *Consciousness and Society* (London : MacGibbon & Kee, 1959), especially chapter 3; George Lichtheim, *Marxism: An Historical and Critical Study* (London : Routledge & Kegan Paul, 1961); and the comprehensive account of one particular Marxist school by Martin Jay, *The Dialectical Imagination: A History of the Frankfurt School and the Institute of Social Research, 1923–1950* (Boston : Little, Brown, 1973).

2. MARXISM AS SOCIOLOGY

In the period from Marx's death in 1883 to the outbreak of the First World War Marxism developed mainly in the form of a science of society. This orientation (although, as I indicated, it could find support in Marx's own views) was imparted above all by Engels, and it is clearly expressed in his 'Speech at the Graveside of Karl Marx', in the claim that: 'Just as Darwin discovered the law of development of organic nature, so Marx discovered the law of development of human history.' Engels' version of the theory, which was largely accepted by Kautsky, then became, under the name of 'scientific socialism', the orthodox doctrine of German Social Democracy and of the Second International.

According to this conception Marxism provided – in terms of changes in the mode of production, the formation of classes and the struggle between classes – a causal explanation of the historical development of human societies, and more particularly of the origins and development of modern capitalism, which could be expressed in the form of historical 'laws'. There could then be deduced from these laws the *necessary* breakdown of capitalism and the transition to socialism. It was in this guise, as a positive science, that Marxism had its impact on sociology in its formative stages, was presented as a system of sociology – that is, as a general and comprehensive science of society – provoked responses from the major sociological thinkers, and in turn was employed in a critical assessment of their ideas. Marxism and other sociological theories appeared as rival schemes of thought, contesting the same terrain.

At the first international congress of sociology, in 1894, several participants expounded the Marxist theory,[1] and a later congress,

[1] *Annales de l'Institut International de Sociologie*, I (Paris: Giard et Brière, 1895). One of the contributors, Enrico Ferri, pub-

in 1900, was largely devoted to a discussion of 'historical material-ism'.[1] In the same period Sorel published a long critical essay on Durkheim's sociology,[2] while in Italy there appeared Labriola's exposition of historical materialism[3] and Croce's essays on the Marxist theory;[4] the latter being distinguished especially by their critical questioning of the conception of Marxism as a scientific theory. The growing significance of Marxism for the develop-ment of sociology can be seen also in the work of the major sociological thinkers. F. Tönnies' *Gemeinschaft und Gesellschaft* (1887),[5] drew heavily upon Marx's analysis of capitalist society. Max Weber, in the greater part of his work, was engaged in a critical confrontation with Marxist thought, in his formulation of an alternative account of the origins of modern capitalism, in his evaluations of the methodological status of the 'economic interpretation of history', and in his researches in the sociology of

---

lished a book entitled *Socialism and Positive Science (Darwin–Spencer–Marx)* (Rome, 1894; English trans. London : Independent Labour Party, 1906), in which he sought to demonstrate that 'Marxian socialism – the only kind that has a positive method and scientific worth . . . is only the practical and fruitful complement in social life of that modern scientific revolution . . . inaugurated several centuries back by the revival of the experimental method in all the branches of human knowledge.'

[1] *Annales,* viii (Paris : Giard et Brière, 1902).

[2] G. Sorel, 'Les Théories de M. Durkheim', *Le Devenir social,* (April–May 1895) 1–26, 148–80. This journal, which Sorel founded and edited during its brief existence from 1895 to 1898, published essays by some of the leading European Marxists and students of Marxist thought, including Engels, Kautsky, Plekhanov, Labriola and Croce; and in its review section discussed much of the new literature of sociology and social history.

[3] Antonio Labriola, *Del materialismo storico* (Rome, 1896). English trans. under the title *Essays on the Materialistic Conception of History* (Chicago : Charles Kerr, 1908).

[4] Written between 1895 and 1899, and published in a volume under the title *Materialismo storico ed economia marxistica,* English trans. of part, ed. A. D. Lindsay, *Historical Materialism and the Economics of Karl Marx* (London : Howard Latimer, 1913).

[5] English trans., *Community and Association* (London : Rout-ledge & Kegan Paul, 1955).

religion which he described as a 'positive criticism of the materialist conception of history'.[1] Pareto, in his *Systèmes socialistes* (1902), made a systematic analysis of the Marxist theory, separating out those elements, such as the idea of class conflict, which he would later incorporate, in a different form, in his own sociological system. Durkheim provided space in the first volume of the *Année sociologique* for reviews of several Marxist works (including his own review of the book by E. Grosse on the forms of the family and economy), though subsequently there was little reference to Marxist writing; and in his course of lectures on socialism – abandoned before reaching the point at which Marx's theory would have been examined – there are some general allusions which indicate that Durkheim saw the closeness of the relation between Marxism and sociology, and thus indirectly envisaged the Marxist thinkers as his principal antagonists : '. . . . in more recent times [socialism] has more and more assumed a certain scientific cast. It is incontestable that in so doing it has perhaps helped social science more than it has been helped by it. For it has awakened reflection; it has stimulated scientific activity, instigated research, posed problems, to such an extent that in more than one respect its history merges with that of sociology.'[2]

But Marxism conceived as a scientific theory of social development faced two major difficulties, which were noted by its critics, and became the subject of debate among Marxists themselves in the 'revisionist' controversy initiated by the publication of Bernstein's *Die Voraussetzungen des Sozialismus und die Aufgaben der Sozialdemokratie*[3] in 1899. In the first place, if Marxism is a positive science its conclusions must be founded ultimately upon some test of experience, some adequate depiction of social facts. One part of Bernstein's argument consisted in saying that the trends of development in the Western capitalist societies were diverging from those formulated by Marx, and that the theory needed to be modified to take account of the recent changes. In

[1] On the relation between Marx and Weber, see especially Karl Löwith, 'Max Weber und Karl Marx' (1932), which is due to appear in an English translation shortly.

[2] Emile Durkheim, *Le Socialisme* (Paris : F. Alcan, 1928) pp. 3–4.

[3] English trans. under the title *Evolutionary Socialism* (New York : Schocken Books, 1961).

notes that were found among his papers Bernstein summarised his view as follows: 'Peasants do not sink; middle class does not disappear; crises do not grow ever larger; misery and serfdom do not increase. There *is* increase in insecurity, dependence, social distance, social character of production, functional superfluity of property owners.'

Bernstein examined in some detail the economic and political changes which, in his view, made it necessary to consider revising the Marxist theory.[1] The single most important element in this part of his study concerned the changing class structure. In his view, the polarisation of classes anticipated by Marx was not occurring; the concentration of capital in large enterprises was accompanied by a development of new small- and medium-sized businesses; property ownership was becoming more widespread; the general level of living was rising; the middle class was increasing rather than diminishing in number; the structure of capitalist society was not being simplified, but was becoming more complex and differentiated. From this analysis Bernstein went on to consider the question of crises and the theory of capitalist 'breakdown', and here he argued that crises were becoming less severe, the periods of prosperity longer, because of various countervailing influences which helped to moderate trade fluctuations and overcome in part the anarchy of the market. Nevertheless, as he pointed out, the trade cycle continued in a less severe form, and a general insecurity remained, which could never be fully overcome in the capitalist system. The political conclusions that Bernstein drew from his analysis were that the transition to socialism would take place, not in dramatic struggles between the polarised classes of bourgeoisie and proletariat, but in a more gradual fashion, by the permeation of capitalism with socialist institutions brought into existence by the working-class movement and its allies in other groups of the population.

The controversies which ensued, and notably Kautsky's response on the question of crises, were disappointing from the aspect of the scientific standing of Marx's theory inasmuch as the orthodox Marxists concentrated their attention mainly upon defending

[1] There is a useful analysis and assessment of Bernstein's views in Peter Gay, *The Dilemma of Democratic Socialism* (New York: Columbia University Press, 1952).

the revolutionary core of the doctrine against reformism; that is to say, upon an issue which was not one of science, but of political commitment. Indeed, the term 'revisionism' itself, in the pejorative sense that it was given, was entirely misleading from a scientific perspective; for the Marxist theory, if it constituted an empirical science of society, must clearly be amenable to continuous criticism resulting from new discoveries and new ideas. In that sense 'revisionism' would be the highest virtue rather than the greatest crime.

The themes that Bernstein broached have remained at the centre of the controversies about Marxist sociology for the past seventy years. The broad issue which they raised, and still raise, is that of an adequate sociological analysis of modern capitalism.[1] Economic development, continuing changes in the occupational and class structure, political upheavals, have reinforced some earlier trends and have produced new social phenomena to be investigated and assessed – the real improvement in the condition of the working class in terms of consumption, work and leisure, along with the maintenance of considerable differences in wealth, prestige and political influence between the principal classes; the continued increase in numbers of the middle class, and the relative decline of the industrial manual workers; the fluctuating and uncertain political role of different classes; the economic stability and steady growth of capitalism during the past thirty years; the enhanced role of the State in economic management; the extension of bureaucratic administration and the rise of the technical expert; the great expansion of social services; and the cultural changes (themselves produced by what forces?) which have given rise to new life styles and new political interests.

From one aspect it might appear easier now to undertake an analysis of these trends, because they have had a longer time in which to establish themselves and to show their real significance.

[1] It is worth noting here that Lukács who, as we shall see, formulated an entirely different version of Marxism in the 1920s, arrived at similar conclusions in one of his last reflections upon the Marxist theory, when he referred to the problem of 'a *real* analysis of the inherent nature of present-day capitalism : a task Marxism has failed to realise so far'. Prefatory note to István Mészáros (ed.), *Aspects of History and Class Consciousness* (London : Routledge & Kegan Paul, 1971).

But I think the difficulties have actually increased. The present-day capitalist societies are even more complex and differentiated, in their occupational and social groupings and in their cultural milieux, than those at the end of the nineteenth century, and so the task of comprehending the interrelationships among their elements is itself more complex and intractable. Moreover, the processes of change continue, but in a very uneven way, and it is far from easy to decide what are, or are likely to become, the dominant trends. A second difficulty arises from the development of sociology itself; almost a century of debate, frequent new departures and just as frequent arrests, have made all too clear how exceedingly slippery are the 'objects' that we attempt to catch in the conceptual and theoretical nets of sociology. The resulting tentativeness of more recent sociological interpretations has a degree of incompatibility with the dogmatic tendencies in Marxist thought (though it is just as incompatible with the dogmatism of behaviourist social scientists, and with some positivist or functionalist derivations from Durkheim's sociology). Finally, a Marxist sociology at the present time would have to be capable of providing not only a 'real' analysis of capitalist society, but also a 'real' analysis of those forms of society which have emerged from revolutions inspired by Marxism itself, but which display many features that are problematic from the standpoint of Marxist theory. I shall return to some of these questions in a later chapter, when I attempt to compare the contributions that Marxism, and other sociological schools, have made to our understanding of recent social trends.

Bernstein, it seems, thought of himself as a positivist; in a much later essay (1924) he wrote : 'My way of thinking would make me a member of the school of Positivist philosophy and sociology. And I would like to have my lecture ["How is Scientific Socialism Possible?"] taken as proof of this attitude of mine. . . .'[1] But although he was close to the positivists in his desire to develop Marxism as an empirical science, he diverged from them in his concern with formulating an ethical theory of socialism, in which he was influenced mainly by the neo-Kantian revival in German

[1] Quoted by Peter Gay, *The Dilemma of Democratic Socialism*, pp. 153–4, footnote.

philosophy. Thus, in one part of his book, Bernstein took up the second major problem of Marxism conceived as an empirical science; namely, that concerning the relation between *is* and *ought*, between socialism as the necessary outcome of capitalist development and socialism as a moral ideal, between objective historical processes and the subjective desires, strivings and ideals of men. But he did not advance very far in the discussion of this subject beyond asserting the existence, and the importance, of an 'ideal' element in the socialist movement.

It was another group of thinkers – the Austro-Marxists[1] – who developed more profoundly the discussion of Marxism as a social science, and of the relation between science and ethics. Otto Bauer described the principal characteristics of the group in the following way:

> What united them was not a specific political orientation, but the particular character of their intellectual work. They had all grown up in a period when men such as Stammler, Windelband and Rickert were attacking Marxism with philosophical arguments; hence they were obliged to engage in controversy with the representatives of modern philosophical trends. If Marx and Engels began from Hegel, and the later Marxists from materialism, the more recent 'Austro-Marxists' had as their point of departure Kant and Mach. On the other side these 'Austro-Marxists' had to engage in controversy with the so-called Austrian school of political economy, and this debate too influenced the method and structure of their thought. Finally, they all had to learn, in the old Austria rent by national struggles, how to apply the Marxist conception of history to very complicated phenomena which defied analysis by any superficial or schematic use of the Marxist method.[2]

[1] The leading intellectual figures were Max Adler, Otto Bauer, Rudolf Hilferding and Karl Renner. Together, in spite of various theoretical and political differences, they formed one of the most notable schools of Marxist thought, the only comparable school being that which was created around the Frankfurt Institute of Social Research. But their work is still much neglected, and very little of it has been translated into English.

[2] Otto Bauer, 'Austro-Marxismus', published anonymously as a leading article in the *Arbeiter-Zeitung* (Vienna, 3 November 1927).

The principal achievements of the Austro-Marxists are to be found in their analysis of the logic of Marxism as a sociological theory, and in their extension of Marxist research to new phenomena and new spheres of social life. Max Adler, the philosopher of the group, argued that Marx had established the basis of a scientific sociology with his conception of 'socialised mankind', which made it possible to bring both nature and society within the scope of a system of causal explanation; and at the same time, that this Marxist sociology was quite compatible with Kantian philosophy, since Marx's theory was a 'critique', in Kant's sense, which established the categories through which man's social being could be understood.[1] But Adler was not prepared to accept the Kantian distinction between a world of causally determined natural or social events and a world of autonomous, self-determined moral judgements; and he did not agree, therefore, with those neo-Kantians who argued that Marxism as a positive science needed to be complemented by a moral philosophy. Instead he claimed that in Marx's theory science and ethics are merged :

> The causal mechanism of history is transformed directly, by the scientific illumination of it, into a teleology, without suffering thereby any breach in its causally determined character. It is simply that the scientific knowledge of a particular social situation now enters as a cause into this causal mechanism. . . . From this point of view there emerges at last . . . the possibility of realizing an age-old desire of philosophy . . . the ideal of a scientifically based politics . . . a scientific technique of social life.[2]

This proposed reconciliation of science and ethics will be examined more closely in a later chapter; here I want to concentrate upon Adler's formulation of the principles of a Marxist sociology. In a later work, which was intended as a systematic exposition of the Marxist theory,[3] Adler set out more fully his

[1] See especially the exposition of this view in his monograph *Der soziologische Sinn der Lehre von Karl Marx* (Leipzig : C. L. Hirschfeld, 1914).

[2] Ibid. p. 25.

[3] Two volumes were published under the title *Lehrbuch der materialistischen Geschichtsauffassung* (Vienna, 1930–2). These

24

view of the materialist conception of history as a scheme of causal explanation, while discussing in greater detail the complexities of social causation, the nature of motives as causes, and the peculiar difficulties encountered in trying to establish precise causal connections in many complex situations. He also analysed more thoroughly the notion of 'socialisation' or 'socialised man', which he took to be the fundamental sociological concept in Marx's thought, and posed the Kantian question (which Simmel posed in a similar form) : 'How is socialisation (society) possible?'; but he made the additional important observation that just as Kant's question about how nature is possible for human consciousness was formulated after the development of Newtonian science, so the question about the possibility of society was posed after Marx's construction of a causal theory of social processes.

Adler's conception of Marxism as a scientific theory was broadly shared by all the Austro-Marxists, who saw their main task as the development of the theory by means of empirical research and a critical confrontation with other economic and sociological doctrines. But although they maintained this scientific and critical attitude, they were not 'revisionists' in the manner of Bernstein; indeed, one of their first published statements (in 1901) was an attack on this kind of revision of Marxism, and a major critical study of Bernstein's views was published by the American Marxist, Louis Boudin, who was closely associated with the Austro-Marxists (and in fact invented this term to describe the school).[1] At least in the earlier period, up to the First World War, they were not particularly concerned with those developments in capitalism (for example, the changing class structure) which could be interpreted as justifying Bernstein's advocacy of reformist politics, but rather with the concentration of capital, the growth of imperialism and international rivalries, and various specific problems which had not been treated at length by Marx; among them the social

volumes have been republished, together with a third volume which had remained in manuscript, under the general title *Soziologie des Marxismus* (Vienna : Europäische Verlagsanstalt, 1964).

[1] Louis Boudin, *The Theoretical System of Karl Marx in the Light of Recent Criticism* (Chicago, 1907; reprinted New York : Monthly Review Press, 1967).

significance, in relation to the working-class movement, of national struggles and nationalism, or the precise relationship between the economic structure and particular ideological 'superstructures' such as the legal system.

Hilferding, in his massive study *Das Finanzkapital*,[1] which was sub-titled 'A study on the most recent development of capitalism', analysed the concentration of corporate ownership, the merging of industrial and banking capital, the attempts to establish control over the whole economy through cartels and trusts, the consequent growth of protectionism, the intensification of economic and political conflict between the capitalist nations, and the development of colonialism as a means of extending the area of economic exploitation by national monopolies.[2] Bauer's book on the problem of nationalities in the Austro-Hungarian Empire,[3] which discussed the nature of national cultures and took up again the Marxist analysis of the 'Jewish question', also led on to a theory of imperialism, which Bauer saw as the outcome of economic depressions and the search for new and more profitable areas for investment.

Another original line of inquiry was that of Karl Renner, who published in 1904 his study of legal institutions in which he attempted to develop a Marxist theory of law which would include, besides the formal analysis of legal norms, an empirical investigation of 'the two adjoining provinces, the origin and the social function of the law': 'Both at the beginning and at the end of legal analysis there is a social theory of the law which correlates it to all non-legal elements of our life, co-ordinating it like a cog to the whole machinery of social events.'[4]

[1] (Vienna, 1910). Only now, more than sixty years later, is the publication of an English translation of this important work projected.

[2] There is a useful discussion of Hilferding's work, in relation to the theories of Lenin, Rosa Luxemburg and Schumpeter, in George Lichtheim, *Imperialism* (New York : Praeger, 1971) chapter 7.

[3] *Die Nationalitätenfrage und die Sozialdemokratie* (Vienna : Marx-Studien, 2, 1907).

[4] *Die soziale Funktion der Rechtsinstitute, besonders des Eigentums* (Vienna, 1904; rev. edn 1928). English trans. with introduction and notes by Otto Kahn-Freund, under the title *The*

26

In their later works the Austro-Marxists did turn to other problems, including that which was posed by the changes in, and new interpretations of, the class structure of capitalist societies. Max Adler, in two articles on the working class published in 1933,[1] examined, in the light of the failure of four years of economic crisis to produce a more revolutionary outlook in the European working class, the significance of increasing social differentiation, and the development of a 'labour aristocracy', which he identified with the bureaucracy of labour organisations (as Michels had done earlier). Renner introduced some new elements into the Marxist theory of class, while insisting that he continued to employ the Marxist 'method', in two essays which were published post-humously.[2] In the first place, Renner analysed the growth of a new class of managers and salaried employees which he called the 'service class'; argued that in the developed capitalist societies the two principal classes were the service class and the working class; and suggested that these two classes were moving closer together and even tending to amalgamate. Hence, these societies were characterised by the presence of non-antagonistic classes and by the absence of any clearly defined ruling class. Secondly, in his general discussion of the problem of class, Renner sketched a more thoroughgoing revision of the Marxist theory when he argued that there had been other kinds of domination and exploitation besides that carried on by classes formed on the basis of property ownership, and that the Marxist school had failed to 'investigate systematically . . . all historical and possible relations of authority.'[3]

Institutions of Private Law and their Social Functions (London : Routledge & Kegan Paul, 1949) pp. 54–5.

[1] 'Wandlung der Arbeiterklasse', *Der Kampf* (September, October 1933).

[2] Karl Renner, *Wandlungen der modernen Gesellschaft: zwei Abhandlungen über die Probleme der Nachkriegszeit* (Vienna : Wiener Volksbuchhandlung, 1953).

[3] This theme was developed later, in the light of experience in the socialist societies of Eastern Europe, by Stanislaw Ossowski, *Class Structure in the Social Consciousness* (London : Routledge & Kegan Paul, 1963); and in a more general way by Ralf Dahrendorf, *Class and Class Conflict in Industrial Society* (London : Routledge & Kegan Paul, 1959).

After the war the Austro-Marxists also turned their attention to some new phenomena. They analysed the post-war revolutions and the characteristics and outcome of the Russian Revolution, and tried to evaluate the policies and practices of revolutionary movements in relation to democracy; and the theme of democracy assumed increasing importance in their studies with the rise of the Nazi movement in Germany and Austria. In the same context, of revolution and democracy, they investigated the growth and functioning, in the immediate post-war period, of 'workers' councils', on which Max Adler published a short book.[1] These studies, which deal with problems in the sphere where social theory and political action are closely interconnected, will be considered again in a later chapter.

It is questionable whether the development of a Marxist sociology has yet progressed much beyond the stage that was reached in the 'revisionist' controversies and in the studies of the Austro-Marxists. Bukharin published in 1921 a textbook exposition of Marxist sociology,[2] which had among its more interesting features the attempt to discuss critically the ideas of other sociologists – including Max Weber and Robert Michels – instead of moving entirely within the circle of Marxist literature. The most forceful presentation of Marxism as a positive, and even behaviourist, science is probably Otto Neurath's monograph on empirical sociology,[3] in which the influence of the Austro-Marxists and the Vienna Circle merged. According to Neurath : 'Of all the attempts at creating a strictly scientific unmetaphysical physicalist sociology, Marxism is the most complete' (p. 349). He went on to criticise the 'metaphysical countercurrents', among them the method of *verstehen*, which opposed the development of an empirical Marxist sociology; and then outlined the principal features of what he called 'sociology on a materialist foundation', in which the task of the sociologist is to discover the laws '. . . of highly

[1] *Demokratie und Rätesystem* (Vienna : Sozialistiche Bücherei Brand, 1919).

[2] English trans. N. Bukharin, *Historical Materialism: A System of Sociology* (New York : International Publishers, 1925).

[3] *Empirische Soziologie: Der wissenschaftliche Gehalt der Geschichte und Nationalökonomie* (Vienna, 1931). English trans. in Otto Neurath, *Empiricism and Sociology*, ed. Marie Neurath and Robert S. Cohen (Dordrecht : Reidel, 1973) pp. 319–421.

complicated social machines in action, and then, if possible these laws have to be reduced to laws of elementary relationships' (p. 371). Marxism has provided the framework for such a sociology, by describing 'the whole structure of an age as a historical formation with special laws conditioned by the situation of the time' (p. 358). Another important study of Marxist sociology was the book contributed by Karl Korsch to a series on modern sociologists,[1] but it will be convenient to examine this later, in the context of Korsch's development from a philosophical to a more sociological conception of Marxism.

In the main, however, the sociological researches and themes that had been initiated at the beginning of the century were not systematically pursued, and the whole domain that might have been occupied by a Marxist sociology was in fact taken over by other schools of sociology, especially in the period of rapid expansion of sociological studies after the Second World War. Of course, Marxism remained as a shadowy or unseen protagonist in much of the writing on social stratification or on social change and conflict; and it had a more direct influence in such studies as those already mentioned, by Ossowski and Dahrendorf, on the class structure, in the work of Georges Friedmann on industrial sociology, in the analysis of classes and élites by C. Wright Mills and others, in the sociological theory of Georges Gurvitch, and to some extent in an analysis of the development of law like that of W. G. Friedmann, *Law and a Changing Society*,[2] which may be seen as continuing the work of Renner. But it is only in the last few years that more distinctive forms of Marxist sociology have emerged again with the renewal of debates about industrial society and neo-capitalism, the new studies of imperialism in relation to what are called the 'developing countries', and the interest provoked by the revival of radical political movements.

There were a number of reasons for the failure to develop a comprehensive Marxist sociology. One general reason is that suggested by Marxist theory itself; namely, the dominance in the culture, and especially in the educational system, of the ideas of

[1] Karl Korsch, *Karl Marx* (London : Chapman & Hall, 1938). A revised edition of the German text, edited by Götz Langkau, has been published : *Karl Marx* (Frankfurt : Europäische Verlagsanstalt, 1967).

[2] (London : Stevens, 1959.)

the ruling class. This phenomenon, the maintenance of capitalist society through the reproduction of bourgeois culture, obviously needs to be investigated in detail,[1] but there is much evidence, at least, of the obstacles that have been put in the way of Marxist social science in the universities of many Western countries. One particularly important influence of this kind was the establishment of the Nazi régime in Germany, which put an end to both Marxism and sociology in a society where the intellectual conditions were exceptionally favourable to the growth of a Marxist sociology.

Nevertheless, this reason alone does not seem to me sufficient to account for the failure. Another major influence was the creation of a powerful Marxist orthodoxy, which claimed to be a social science but was no more than a political dogma, in the U.S.S.R. and throughout the international communist movement; for several decades this 'official' doctrine inhibited any serious thought or research. Finally, we have to take account of those intellectual movements in Western Europe, and especially in Germany, which led Marxist thinkers away from the idea of Marxism as a social science toward a reaffirmation of its philosophical and Hegelian constituents.

[1] The recent writings of Pierre Bourdieu make an important contribution to this field of study, but there are also wider issues about the degree to which the culture of the present-day Western societies can properly be described as 'bourgeois'. There are some interesting reflections on this question in Norman Birnbaum, *The Crisis of Industrial Society* (New York : Oxford University Press, 1969).

3. MARXISM AGAINST SOCIOLOGY

The reaction against the conception of Marxism as a positive science was affected by intellectual trends but also by political circumstances. As Stuart Hughes has observed,[1] the revolt against positivism had already developed strongly during the decade of the 1890s, and its influence soon extended to Marxist thought. Croce, even during the brief period of his interest in Marxism, had conceived it as a method of historical interpretation, profoundly connected with Hegel's philosophy, and not as a general social science. Sorel, after initially taking the side of Bernstein in the 'revisionist' controversy,[2] later presented Marxism as the theory of revolutionary syndicalism,[3] but there was always a certain consistency in his view. What he praised in Bernstein's work was not only the effort to observe and describe the real world, but also its activist orientation, its invitation to socialists to play a 'truly effective role' in the world, and above all its emphasis on the moral element in socialism. For Sorel was always critical of the idea of historical inevitability, and argued that socialism is primarily a moral doctrine, bringing to the world 'a new manner of judging all human acts' or, to use Nietzsche's expression, 'a transvaluation of all values'; it 'confronts the bourgeois world as an irreconcilable adversary, threatening it with a moral catastrophe much more than with a material catastrophe'.[4] This em-

[1] H. Stuart Hughes, *Consciousness and Society* (London : MacGibbon & Kee, 1959) chapter 2.

[2] Georges Sorel, 'Les Polémiques pour l'interprétation du Marxisme', *Revue internationale de sociologie* (Paris, 1900).

[3] See especially *Réflexions sur la violence* (Paris : Marcel Rivière, 1908).

[4] Preface to Saverio Merlino, *Formes et essence du socialisme* (Paris, 1898).

phasis upon the practical, revolutionary side of Marx's thought also characterised Lenin's response to 'revisionism' and to the whole scientific, evolutionist tendency of German Marxism; but Lenin's activism was directly political, concerned with changing the world, not with reinterpreting in any profound way either the world or Marxism.

Among the post-war generation of Marxist thinkers a conception of Marxism as a 'critical philosophy' or a 'philosophy of *praxis*' eventually became predominant, expressed in diverse ways by Korsch, Lukács, Gramsci and the philosophers of the Frankfurt Institute of Social Research (particularly Horkheimer and Marcuse). Apart from the intellectual influences upon them – the various anti-positivist doctrines stemming from Dilthey's conception of a 'science of the spirit' relying upon a hermeneutic understanding of history, from phenomenology, from the *Lebensphilosophie*, and in Italy from the idealist philosophy of history of Croce and Gentile – they were also profoundly affected by political events. The Russian Revolution showed how a small revolutionary party, armed with Marxist doctrine, could intervene effectively and change the course of events, while the failure of the working class in Western Europe to develop a revolutionary outlook, either in the immediate post-war period or in the 1930s, taught a similar lesson; namely, that a revolutionary consciousness, embodied in an activist interpretation of Marxism, had to be brought to the working class from outside. The growth of the Nazi and Fascist movements, and the ineffectualness of working-class resistance to them, seemed to confirm the view that it was erroneous, and dangerous, to envisage the spontaneous development of a socialist outlook in the working class, and eventually in some sections of the middle class (as Bernstein had suggested), or an inevitable transition to socialism. At the same time the success of these movements also posed new problems, which began to be studied in the 1930s by some of the associates of the Frankfurt Institute, and led to other divergences in the evaluation of Marxist social theory.

Lukács's Marxism, as it was formulated in the essays collected in *History and Class Consciousness*,[1] and as it continued to direct

[1] First published Berlin, *Geschichte und Klassenbewusstsein*, 1923. English trans. London : The Merlin Press, 1971.

his thinking in spite of recantations on certain points,[1] displayed many of these influences. It was based upon two main ideas. The first is that the truth about history is to be discovered by a rational insight into the historical process, not by empirical, sociological investigations. This contrast between sociology and Marxism (characterised by its dialectical method) is well expressed in Lukács's critical review of Bukharin's textbook, where he refers to Bukharin's 'false methodology', his 'conception of Marxism as a "General Sociology" ', and continues :

> ... as a necessary consequence of his natural-scientific approach, sociology cannot be restricted to a pure method, but develops into an independent science with its own goals. The dialectic can do without such independent substantive achievements; its realm is that of the historical process as a whole, whose individual, concrete, unrepeatable moments reveal its dialectical essence precisely in the qualitative differences between them and in the continuous transformation of their objective structure. The *totality* is the territory of the dialectic.[2]

The second fundamental idea is that in the epoch of capitalism an adequate or true insight into the historical process is attained only by the proletariat, because of its position in society; and this insight is formulated rationally and systematically in the Marxist theory, which can therefore be regarded as identical with the class consciousness of the proletariat. But since the actual consciousness of workers takes diverse forms, is not predominantly revolutionary, and does not embody, except in a minority of instances, the Marxist view of history, Lukács had to make a distinction between this actual 'psychological' consciousness and

[1] Only towards the end of his life did Lukács question more fundamentally his whole interpretation of the Marxist theory when, in his preface to the new edition of *History and Class Consciousness* (1967), he noted self-critically the 'revolutionary, utopian messianism' expressed in these essays and referred to his uncertainty about the essential content and methodological validity of Marxism as he had expounded it.

[2] Published in 1925. English trans, under the title 'Technology and Social Relations', *New Left Review*, XXXIX (1966).

an 'imputed rational consciousness' which would correspond with the Marxist theory. This process of 'imputation', however, is the work of intellectuals, of Marxist thinkers; hence Marxism is, after all, a particular interpretation of history which, if its superiority is not to be dogmatically asserted simply on the grounds that it is conceived from the 'standpoint of the working class', must seek to establish its validity in some rational or empirical way against other interpretations. The question of the relation between the Marxist theory of the working class in capitalist society and the actual empirical development of working-class organisations and working-class political consciousness has been crucially important, as we have seen, in the twentieth-century controversies about Marxism; and it is a question that Lukács never really faced.[1]

Gramsci's view of Marxism, and of its relation to sociology, was similar in many respects to that of Lukács; and again it received one of its clearest formulations in a critical essay on Bukharin's textbook :

. . . what does it mean to say that the philosophy of praxis is a sociology? What sort of thing would this sociology be? A science of politics and historiography? Or a systematic collection, classified in a particular ordered form, of purely empirical observations on the art of politics and of external canons of historical research? . . . is not sociology an attempt to produce a so-called exact (i.e. positivist) science of social facts, that is of politics and history – in other words a philosophy in embryo? Has not sociology tried to do something similar to the philosophy of praxis? . . . Sociology has been an attempt to create a method of historical and political science in a form dependent on a pre-elaborated philosophical system, that of evolutionist positivism, against which sociology reacted, but only partially. . . . It is therefore an attempt to derive 'experimentally' the laws of evolution of human society in such a way as to 'predict' that the oak tree will develop out of the acorn. Vulgar evolutionism is at the root of sociology, and sociology cannot

[1] I have discussed the problems raised by Lukács's account of class consciousness more fully in an essay on 'Class Structure and Social Consciousness', reprinted in Tom Bottomore, *Sociology as Social Criticism* (London : Allen & Unwin, 1974) chapter 7.

know the dialectical principle with its passage from quantity to quality. But this passage disturbs any form of evolution and any law of uniformity understood in a vulgar evolutionist sense.[1]

However, Gramsci did not elaborate this notion of a dialectical principle or method; he did not show its value in any sustained investigation of a specific sequence of events; and he did not offer any substantial analysis of an explanation or interpretation provided by modern sociology in such a way as to bring out clearly its supposed limitations and defects.[2] What he did was to formulate a very general criticism to the effect that sociology has not produced any genuine 'laws' (which is a platitude found in every critical discussion of positivist sociology); and to outline, in a particular form, the problem of the relation between knowledge and society (which has also become a commonplace in controversies within sociology) by arguing that: 'With the extension of mass parties and their organic coalescence with the intimate (economic–productive) life of the masses themselves, the process whereby popular feeling is standardised ceases to be mechanical and causal (that is produced by the conditioning of environmental factors and the like) and becomes conscious and critical.'[3]

Gramsci's main purpose was to present Marxism as a philosophical world view. The fundamental concept of orthodox Marxism, he claims, is that '. . . the philosophy of praxis is "sufficient unto itself", that it contains in itself all the fundamental elements needed to construct a total and integral conception of the world, a total philosophy and theory of natural science,

[1] 'Critical Notes on an Attempt at Popular Sociology', in Quintin Hoare and Geoffrey Nowell Smith (eds), *Selections from the Prison Notebooks of Antonio Gramsci* (London : Lawrence & Wishart, 1971) pp. 419–72, especially p. 426.

[2] This comment has a wider bearing. It is a curious, and indeed absurd, feature of much Hegelian-Marxist criticism of sociology that it concentrates upon the differences between Marx's theory and Comte's 'positive philosophy' (which played little part in the subsequent development of sociology) while ignoring all the major works of modern sociology. This is the case, as we shall see, in the earlier writings of Korsch and notably in the work of Marcuse.

[3] *Selections from the Prison Notebooks*, p. 429.

and not only that but everything that is needed to give life to an integral practical organization of society, that is, to become a total integral civilization'.[1] Before considering more fully at a later stage the criticisms that can be brought against these ideas, which diverge so widely from the intention of Marx's own thought (it was perhaps just in this sense that he declared he was 'not a Marxist'), it may be useful to make one general comment. It is much more doubtful now than it was when Gramsci wrote whether Marxism is actually capable of accomplishing this grandiose mission to provide the intellectual and cultural elements of a new civilisation. In the socialist countries in which Marxism is the official ideology it seems to be accepted at best with grudging acquiescence rather than with the enthusiasm aroused by a new moral vision; and practical social life seems to be directed by much the same values (centred upon the material conditions of life, careers, leisure activities) as prevail in the Western societies. On the other side, Marxism has brought into existence in many of the socialist countries, whether fortuitously or not, conditions of political oppression and cultural impoverishment which represent, in the eyes of many observers, a notable decline from a level of civilisation previously attained. Hence it seems more plausible to say that it is 'socialism', in its diverse forms, rather than Marxism as a 'total' philosophy, which has carried within itself, up to now, the elements of a new civilisation.

Although Gramsci wanted to distinguish sharply between Marxism as a world view and sociology as a social science he did not deny all value to the latter as 'an empirical compilation of practical observations' which, in the form of statistics, would provide, for instance, a basis for planning.[2] In the work of Korsch, who also began by presenting Marxism in a philosophical form – in a manner very similar to that of Lukács[3] – by

[1] Ibid. p. 462.
[2] Ibid. pp. 428–9. It is mainly in this form, as the compilation of survey data, that sociology has developed in the socialist countries.
[3] Karl Korsch, *Marxism and Philosophy* (*Marxismus und Philosophie*, Leipzig, 1923; English trans., London : New Left Books, 1970). In a brief postscript Korsch referred to Lukács's *History and Class Consciousness*, which appeared just as his own book was going to press, and spoke of his 'fundamental agreement' with its themes,

arguing that Marxism as a materialist philosophy was the theoretical expression of the revolutionary proletariat, just as German idealist philosophy had been the theoretical expression of the revolutionary bourgeoisie,[1] sociology and the sociological elements in Marxism gradually acquired a greater prominence. In an essay published in 1937[2] Korsch undertook to examine the 'relationship between Marxism and modern sociological teaching', but after briefly dismissing Comte, and characterising the 'sociology of the nineteenth and twentieth centuries which originated with Comte and was propagated by Mill and Spencer' as a 'reaction against modern socialism', he scarcely mentioned any modern sociological studies. What he did was to formulate four basic principles of Marxism as 'the genuine social science of our time' and as a practical instrument of working-class struggle : (1) the principle of historical specification – 'Marx comprehends all things social in terms of a definite historical epoch'; (2) the principle of concrete application – this seems to refer to the empirical basis of Marxist criticism of the bourgeois family, property relations, and so on; (3) the principle of revolutionary change – in opposition to evolutionist theories; and (4) the principle of revolutionary practice – the attempt through analysis and criticism to discover the main tendencies of further social development and to make possible a conscious rational involvement in the historical process.

In his major work, *Karl Marx*, Korsch elaborated these principles and indicated more plainly the new direction that his ideas had taken, away from the predominantly philosophical concerns of fifteen years earlier :

In the subsequent development of Marxism, the critical materialist principle that Marx had worked out empirically . . . was

---

but in a later essay published as an introduction to the second edition of his book (1930) he emphasised the divergences between himself and Lúkacs, though without discussing how far their political differences were connected with theoretical disagreements.

[1] *Marxism and Philosophy*, p. 42.
[2] 'Leading Principles of Marxism : A Restatement', *Marxist Quarterly*, 1, 3 (October–December 1937); reprinted in Karl Korsch, *Three Essays on Marxism* (London : Pluto Press, 1971).

elaborated into a general social philosophy. . . . From this distortion of the strongly empirical and critical sense of the materialistic principle it was only a step to the idea that the historical and economic science of Marx must be based on the broader foundation not only of a social philosophy, but even of a comprehensive materialist philosophy embracing both nature and society, or a general philosophical interpretation of the universe.[1]

And in the final chapter he summed up his view thus :

The main tendency of historical materialism is no longer 'philosophical', but is that of an empirical scientific method. It provides the starting point for a real solution of the problem that naturalistic materialism and positivism, because of their eclectic introduction of natural science methods into social science, only appeared to solve.[2]

The most important substantive element in the book is Korsch's emphasis upon the analysis of all social phenomena in their relation to the economy, and the conception of the economy as a historical phenomenon, as Marx's major contribution to social science. In a passage intended for a subsequent revision of his book Korsch argued indeed that the principal distinction between sociology and Marxist social theory was to be found in the fact that sociology treats the system of social relations as an autonomous sphere of inquiry, whereas Marxism approaches it from the standpoint of a prior analysis of the economy: *'To this extent, Marx's materialistic science of society is not sociology, but political economy.'*[3] This has remained one of the important issues in all subsequent Marxist criticism of sociology. However, it must be said that Korsch outlined the Marxist theory of society in a very abstract way, and he paid little attention to such empirical matters as the actual development of capitalism in the twentieth century and the problems that might be posed – and were posed by Bernstein

[1] *Karl Marx*, rev. German edn, p. 145.
[2] Ibid. p. 203.
[3] Ibid. p. 277.

and the Austro-Marxists – concerning the changes in the economic structure or in the class system. Indeed Korsch made no reference at all to the Austro-Marxists, to Bernstein's ideas, or to any recent economic or sociological studies; Marxism, in this exposition, is quite distinctly a mid-nineteenth-century doctrine, defined mainly by contrast with the political economy of Adam Smith and Ricardo.

Later on, Korsch abandoned Marxism altogether, though without subjecting it to a systematic criticism;[1] and he seemed to return to a philosophical view of society, but one which had a more personal, subjective character. In notes prepared for a lecture tour in Europe in 1950 and circulated in mimeographed form under the title 'Ten Theses on Marxism Today',[2] he asserted that : 'It makes no sense any longer to pose the question how far the theory of Marx and Engels is still theoretically valid and capable of practical application. All attempts to re-establish the Marxist theory as a whole, and in its original function as a theory of the working-class social revolution, are now reactionary utopias.' But he then went on to formulate what he regarded as the first step in the 'reconstruction of a revolutionary theory and praxis'. This desire for a new revolutionary theory and political activity, however, is no longer embedded in a scheme of thought which provides (as Marxism did) a systematic theory of society or a comprehensive philosophical world view; it seems to arise simply from an individual (and in Hegel's sense capricious) moral or philosophical judgement, from a purely subjective reading of human history.

From this aspect the later development of Korsch's thought seems to parallel quite closely that of some of the thinkers associated with the Frankfurt Institute, just as it had a similar starting-point. In fact, Korsch took part in the 'First Marxist Work Week', held in 1922, from which the Frankfurt Institute developed, and much of the discussion at this first meeting was devoted to his forth-

[1] During his last years Korsch was working on a comprehensive summing-up of his views on Marxist theory, but illness prevented him from completing it. (I am indebted to Mrs Hedda Korsch for this information.)

[2] Subsequently published in French, in *Arguments*, 16 (1959), and in German, in *Alternative*, 41 (1965).

coming book *Marxism and Philosophy*.[1] This book, and Lukács's *History and Class Consciousness*, provided the main stimulus within Marxist thought to the development of a particular philosophical form of Marxism, distinguished on one side from the official metaphysical doctrine of 'dialectical materialism' or 'Marxism–Leninism', and on the other side from positivist social science (although in the early years a number of the Institute's members – Grünberg, Wittfogel, Grossman – retained a more positivist approach). As Lichtheim has observed : '. . . what we have here is not so much a rediscovery of the authentic core of Marxism as a revival of a philosophical tradition which can properly be called Hegelian.'[2]

The most influential thinkers of the Frankfurt Institute – Horkheimer, Adorno and Marcuse – reverted to the concerns of the Young Hegelians of the 1840s; above all, they emphasised the importance of the subjective element in practical activity, attributed a greater autonomy and significance to the cultural superstructure, and devoted their main efforts to the elaboration of the kind of 'critical criticism' that Marx had derided. Of course, there were also considerable differences between the situation of the 1840s and that of the 1930s. Many other intellectual currents had appeared which drew upon Hegel's philosophy and engaged in a critique of positivism; and there had been great economic and political changes – especially the development of the social and political system of the U.S.S.R., and the rise of Fascism – which presented quite new problems for critical reflection. But there is one feature in particular which

[1] Jay, *The Dialectical Imagination*, p. 5. After the first few years, however, Korsch had little or no connection with the work of the Institute, partly because he was more deeply engaged in political activity than were most of its members, partly because his theoretical interests, as we have seen, moved from a philosophical towards a more scientific conception of Marxism during the 1930s.

[2] George Lichtheim, *From Marx to Hegel* (London : Orbach & Chambers, 1971) p. 2. The first essay in this volume provides an excellent account of the conditions which encouraged the growth of a Hegelianised Marxism during the 1930s, and again after 1945 when the influences of Hegel's philosophy and of phenomenology were given a new lease of life in existentialism.

links the Frankfurt philosophers with the Young Hegelians, namely, the absence of the working class. Marx had gone beyond the Young Hegelians in formulating a philosophy of *praxis*, a conception of practical–critical activity, through his discovery of the proletariat as a material force in social life in which revolutionary activity and theoretical criticism were, or would become, united. The Frankfurt thinkers confronted a situation in which, as they thought, the working class had ceased to be revolutionary; hence they were led back to a pre-Marxist notion of revolutionary activity as the product of a revolutionary 'critical consciousness'. The full impact of this view has only become clear in more recent times, in the later writings of Marcuse, and in the work of the younger generation of thinkers associated with the post-war 'Frankfurt School', which I shall consider shortly.

The criticism of sociology by the Frankfurt philosophers was mainly indirect, through the criticism of positivism, although Marcuse, in *Reason and Revolution,* specifically rejected Comte's sociology in terms which were more widely applicable :

> Social study was to be a science seeking social laws, the validity of which was to be analogous to that of physical laws. Social practice, especially the matter of changing the social system, was herewith throttled by the inexorable. Society was viewed as governed by rational laws that moved with a natural necessity. . . . The positivist repudiation of metaphysics was . . . coupled with a repudiation of man's claim to alter and reorganize his social institutions in accordance with his rational will.[1]

But while the philosophical criticism of positivism was always dominant it did not constitute the whole of the Institute's work, much of which explored new subjects that were obviously important for the development of Marxist social theory. This was especially true of the attempt to bring psychology and psychoanalysis within a Marxist framework, and to make use of these disciplines in an analysis of the new and disturbing phenomenon of Fascism.

[1] H. Marcuse, *Reason and Revolution: Hegel and the Rise of Social Theory* (New York : Oxford University Press, 1941) pp. 343–4.

The studies along these lines were largely inspired by Erich Fromm, who was associated with the Institute from the early 1930s until 1939, when he separated from it mainly because of the declining radicalism of its orientation. Fromm published in the first issue of the Institute's journal, the *Zeitschrift für Sozialforschung* (1932), an essay on 'The Method and Task of an Analytical Social Psychology'[1] in which he argued that psychoanalysis (albeit in a revised form) could enrich the Marxist conception of human nature, and help to provide a more adequate account of the relationship between the economic basis of society and the ideological superstructure. In the study which he published later, on the development of personality in modern society, authoritarianism and the psychology of Nazism, he set out in an appendix his idea of the 'social character', and summed up his views thus :

> Economic forces are effective, but they must be understood not as psychological motivations but as objective conditions; psychological forces are effective, but must be understood as historically conditioned themselves; ideas are effective, but they must be understood as being rooted in the whole of the character structure of members of a social group. . . . In other words, social conditions influence ideological phenomena through the medium of character; character, on the other hand, is not the result of passive adaptation to social conditions but of a dynamic adaptation on the basis of elements that either are biologically inherent in human nature or have become inherent as the result of historic evolution.[2]

Fromm's work had a more positivist and empirical orientation than that of many other members of the Institute; in particular, in recognising that the economic, psychological and ideological forces in society, while interdependent, also had a certain degree of independence, he observed that this is '. . . . particularly true of the economic development which, being dependent on objective factors, such as the natural productive forces, technique,

[1] English trans. in Erich Fromm, *The Crisis of Psychoanalysis* (New York : Holt, Rinehart & Winston, 1970).
[2] *The Fear of Freedom* (London : Routledge & Kegan Paul, 1942) pp. 252–3.

geographical factors, takes place according to its own laws.[1] The general concerns of the Institute, however, became increasingly philosophical, especially after the return to Germany in 1949; the exponents of 'critical theory' now concentrated their attention upon the criticism of mass culture, of what they saw as the negative aspects of Enlightenment rationalism, of the intellectual predominance of scientific and technological thought. To a large extent their ideas merged into the general critique of positivism, which revived the methodological disputes of the late nineteenth century while introducing some new themes, especially from linguistic philosophy;[2] and they gradually lost any distinctive relation to Marxist theory. This movement of thought is most evident in the writings of Marcuse and of some of those – notably Habermas and Wellmer – who may be regarded as the last generation of the Frankfurt School before its virtual dissolution at the end of the 1960s.

In *One-Dimensional Man*[3] Marcuse set out the thesis that in the advanced industrial countries the progress of science and technology has established a form of domination, a system of social control, which, by achieving the social and cultural integration of the working class into society, has eliminated any real force capable of bringing about a radical historical change to a new type of society :

The critical theory of society [i.e. Marxism] was, at the time of its origin, confronted with the presence of real forces . . . *in* the established society which moved (or could be guided to move) toward more rational and freer institutions by abolishing the existing ones which had become obstacles to progress. These were the empirical grounds on which the theory was erected. . . . Without the demonstration of such forces, the critique of society would still be valid and rational, but it would be incapable of translating its rationality into terms of historical practice.

[1] Ibid. p. 253.
[2] See, for instance, Peter Winch, *The Idea of a Social Science and its Relation to Philosophy* (London : Routledge & Kegan Paul, 1958).
[3] (Boston : Beacon Press, 1964.)

And he concludes: 'The critical theory of society possesses no concepts which could bridge the gap between the present and its future; holding no promise and showing no success, it remains negative.'[1] What this reveals is the stubborn commitment of a particular 'critical theorist' to a subjective, arbitrary interpretation of history which is no longer connected either with a social movement or with a publicly accessible body of knowledge and criteria of validity by which its assertions might be judged. It is also a final abandonment of anything that could be called a Marxist theory for it eliminates two indispensable elements of Marxist thought: the conception of the fundamental, 'progressive' significance of the development of the economic system, and in particular of the capitalist economy; and the idea of the working class as a revolutionary force, the unique historical agent and bearer of a new civilisation. In a similar way both Habermas and Wellmer separate themselves from Marxism by their assertion that the importance of social classes has greatly diminished or become negligible in the present-day capitalist societies,[2] by their emphasis upon the cultural superstructure rather than the economic basis as the sphere in which radical changes have to be accomplished, and perhaps most of all by their thoroughgoing criticism of what they see, quite rightly, as the positivist elements in Marx's own theory which in their view invalidate it as a way of studying human society.

Two general features can be discerned in the development of philosophical Marxism in opposition to sociology. The first – most evident in the later work of the Frankfurt School – is the return to a pre-Marxist framework of thought, in the sense that it is closer to Hegel than to Marx. And as Lichtheim remarked 'if we find that contemporary thinking reproduces the problematic of an earlier historical situation – namely that out of which Marxism arose – we are entitled to suppose that it does so because the relationship of theory to practice has once more become the sort of problem it was for Hegel's followers in the 1840's.'[3] I

[1] *One-Dimensional Man*, pp. 254–5.

[2] Wellmer, *Critical Theory of Society*, p. 138, concludes that 'Marx's concept of class has largely lost its utility as an instrument of analysis'.

[3] G. Lichtheim, *From Marx to Hegel* (London: Orbach & Chambers, 1971) p. 14.

shall discuss the whole question of theory and practice in the next chapter, but it will be useful at this point to bring together some of the issues that emerge from the preceding discussion. The development of a Hegelianised Marxism was largely a response to the uncertainties about the theoretical grounding of revolutionary action in the political conditions that appeared in the course of the twentieth century; the collapse of German Social Democracy and the Second International at the outbreak of the First World War (which could be interpreted as a consequence of their 'reformism', and this in turn as the outcome of their scientific, evolutionist version of Marxism); the contrasting success of the Russian Revolution through the actions of a revolutionary *avant-garde*; the apparent decline in the revolutionary commitment of the working class in Western Europe, and on the other side, the growth of activist right-wing movements; the deceptions resulting from the consolidation of the Stalinist régime in the U.S.S.R. (which also justified itself by appealing to Marxism as a 'scientific theory') and its later extension to other societies in Eastern Europe. In a more general way we can say that Marxism as a more or less deterministic theory of social development obviously had a greater appeal when the trend of events actually appeared to be leading towards socialism and it could be confidently asserted that 'history is on our side'. But when the course of history revealed a more disagreeable aspect, in the totalitarian régimes, either Fascist or Stalinist, or in the establishment of what seemed to be a more stable type of inegalitarian welfare-capitalism after 1945, those thinkers who wanted to preserve the revolutionary hope of a transition from capitalism to socialism were pushed towards a different interpretation of Marxism; one which emphasised the subjective elements – revolutionary consciousness and commitment – in practical activity. Of course, this interpretation could still assume various forms : Lukács, Gramsci and Korsch in the early 1920s saw the revolutionary consciousness as embodied in the Communist Party, while the Frankfurt philosophers viewed it rather as an attribute of Marxist intellectuals. But in both these cases, and in others which diverged from them in this or that detail, the same claim was made to the possession of a privileged insight into the truth about history that could be opposed to any merely empirical, sociological account of

47

historical events in all their disturbing nastiness.

The second, very curious, feature in the development of philosophical Marxism is that while it began as a Marxist criticism of sociology it has detached itself more and more from some of the fundamental (and most influential) ideas of Marx's theory, and at the same time has moved closer to the conceptions and methods that are to be found in some recent forms of sociology. In a broad sense there has been a merging of phenomenological Marxism with phenomenological sociology, but in the process something distinctive has been lost. The principal object of criticism, in the sphere of thought, is now the positivist elements in the social sciences, not the bourgeois theories of society, and in the sphere of practical life it is the 'technological society', not capitalism. Indeed these objects of criticism are linked, as were capitalism and bourgeois thought in Marx's theory, for positivism (or 'instrumental reason') is seen as the dominant form of thought generated by technological society and in turn functions as an ideology sustaining and reinforcing the institutions of that society. What is not at all clear – just as it was not clear in the case of the Young Hegelians – is the precise sense in which this post-Marxist 'critical theory' can be regarded as being politically radical or revolutionary. In the 1960s there was a largely fortuitous, and in any case brief, encounter with the radicalism of the student movement; but the main effort has been to understand the world rather than to change it. What began as an activist doctrine seems to have ended, for the time being, in pessimistic contemplation.

4. THEORY AND PRACTICE

The idea of the merging of theory and practice has a central place in Marxist thought. Its origins are to be found in the discussions among the Young Hegelians in the 1840s, and especially in a book published in 1838 by August Cieszkowski, *Prolegomena zur Historiosophie*.[1] Cieszkowski argued that as men had now attained, through Hegel's philosophy, Absolute Knowledge, the next stage in their development could only be the application of this knowledge in order to transform the world :

> . . . philosophy has reached so classical a point that it has to transcend itself and thus to yield up the Universal Empire to another . . . to practical social life. . . . From now on, the absolutely practical, that is, social action and life within the state . . . will be the Ultimate . . . Being and thought have to perish in action, art and philosophy in social life, in order to re-emerge and to unfold in the ultimate form of social life.[2]

Cieszkowski referred to this social practice emerging from Absolute Knowledge as 'post-theoretical practice' or 'praxis' in which the highest conceivable synthesis of being and thought was attained; and the complex of ideas upon which this con-

[1] Cieszkowski's ideas are discussed at some length in Nicholas Lobkowicz, *Theory and Practice* (Notre Dame, New York : University of Notre Dame Press, 1967) chapter 13; and more briefly in David McLellan, *The Young Hegelians and Karl Marx* (London : Macmillan, 1969). Both authors also provide useful general accounts of the intellectual milieu of the Young Hegelians.

[2] Cieszkowski, *Prolegomena*, pp. 101, 112, cited by Lobkowicz, pp. 198–200.

ception was based entered profoundly into Marx's theory[1] and into some of the later developments of Marxism. Thus Cieszkowski made a distinction between 'facts' and 'acts' – the former being those events which human consciousness can only 'explain and transfigure' but not determine, the latter those events which are first reflected upon and then carried out consciously – that obviously corresponds very closely with Marx's distinction between 'pre-history', when men's social life is largely determined by external forces, and the approaching period when men will 'make their own history' consciously and deliberately, by establishing a rational control over nature, including their own nature.

But as Lobkowicz points out, Cieszkowski's treatment of the problems of social practice remained very vague and abstract,[2] and it was only in Marx's work that the ideas he had sketched finally acquired an immense practical, political significance. Marx's great achievement was to construct a social theory which, though it had a universal character as a framework for analysing all human societies, was more particularly a theory of the working class in capitalist society; and at the same time as it explained the development of the working class it also provided a view of society and history which could be absorbed into the consciousness of the working class and guide its political practice. In Marx's theory, therefore, the working class – as a real, identifiable social group, a collective subject – embodies the unity of theory and practice. But this conception can be interpreted in different ways which it is important to distinguish. In Lukács's version of Marxist theory the idea is given a Hegelian form in the definition of the proletariat as the identical subject–object of the historical process, and this also reintroduces Hegel's concept of Absolute Knowledge as knowledge of the ultimate truth about history.[3] This Absolute

[1] There is no evidence that Marx was directly influenced by Cieszkowski's book, but he would have been acquainted with its main ideas through Moses Hess; and in any case, such ideas were widely discussed in the circle of the Young Hegelians. See the comments by Lobkowicz, *Theory and Practice*, pp. 203–6.

[2] Ibid. p. 202.

[3] Much later Lukács himself recognised this, when he noted in his preface to the new edition of *History and Class Consciousness* (Neuwied: Luchterhand Verlag, 1967) that the 'ultimate philo-

Knowledge provides, evidently, an infallible guide to practical activity (as Cieszkowski thought) and the Marxist thinker – either as an individual, or else, as Lucács seems generally to have supposed, in a collective form as the Communist Party – is able, by his possession of it, to determine unerringly what is the correct outlook and political activity of the working class in each historical phase of its development. In a somewhat different form similar ideas provide the basis for Marcuse's doctrine as it is expressed in *One-Dimensional Man*; somehow, the 'critical theorist' is able to set himself up as the supreme judge of the irrationality of existing society and as the final arbiter of the 'genuine' needs of all men.

In Marx's own theory, however, this idea of Absolute Knowledge plays no part, and is indeed subjected to withering criticism as a pure *abstraction*, as the product of the abstract thinker who commits himself to understanding society and history by *intuition*.[1] If then we regard the Marxist theory as having developed in opposition to this idealist conception and method, as an empirical science of society based upon the analysis of material modes of production, we must also consider how far this reorientation of thought implies a different relation between theory and practice . For the knowledge produced by science, far from being 'absolute', is tentative and corrigible, and only to a limited extent can it be regarded as providing an assured foundation for a 'correct' practice. *Praxis* then assumes a different character. It is no longer social practice informed by theory in the sense of a self-conscious, undetermined activity of individuals or social groups arising from a total understanding of the truth about the historical process, but action based upon the partial, corrigible knowledge acquired by empirical study of social structure and

---

sophical foundation' of the book was 'the identical subject–object that realizes itself in the historical process' (Hegel's 'absolute spirit'), and that it was 'an attempt to out-Hegel Hegel . . . an edifice boldly erected above every possible reality'. But he did not proceed nearly far enough in this criticism of the Hegelian elements in his work.

[1] In the *Economic and Philosophical Manuscripts*; see T. B. Bottomore (ed.), *Karl Marx: Early Writings* (London : Watts, 1963) pp. 199–200, 216–17.

historical events. At the same time, practice itself, the actual development of economic, social and political relationships, has to be seen as exercising an influence upon theory, by posing new problems and by bringing into question some of the propositions which constitute, or are derived from, the theory. In short, the problem of *praxis* – of the relation between theory and practice – cannot be treated adequately from the theoretical side alone, as a question that some general theoretical or philosophical scheme might definitively resolve, but must be viewed also from the side of practice, taking account of the changes in theory that may be required by the development of social life in new forms, and by giving due importance to the empirical investigation of *praxis* itself, that is of the socially and historically situated interconnection of theory and practice.

From this point of view Bernstein's study of the changes in capitalism, and many later critical studies, are entirely legitimate inquiries into the problem of *praxis* which ask, not how social practice can be made to conform with some philosophical insight, but how a theoretical system can be developed and revised empirically in order to portray more accurately and explain more adequately the trends in social practice. At the same time these studies raise another question which has been at the heart of the controversies about Marxist *praxis* since the end of the nineteenth century; namely the relation between science and ethics. Those thinkers who took a broadly positivist view and accepted the distinction between fact and value, faced a variety of difficulties in their interpretation of the socialist movement itself. In so far as they conceived history strictly as a causal process they had to regard the socialist movement as a necessary, determined phenomenon, and the transition to a socialist society as inevitable. Hence, moral impulses and aims were irrelevant and socialist politics could be represented (by Kautsky, for example) as an ethically neutral social technology based upon a science of society. Others, however – and notably Bernstein and Vorländer[1] – argued

[1] K. Vorländer, an eminent neo-Kantian philosopher, expounded his version of 'ethical socialism' in *Kant und der Sozialismus* (Berlin, 1900) and provided a comprehensive account of the philosophical ideas of the whole revisionist movement in *Kant und Marx* (Tübingen : J. C. B. Mohr, 1926).

that a Marxist social science needed to be complemented by an ethical theory if socialism were to be shown as morally superior and therefore worth striving for as an end. But this juxtaposition of a social science and an ethical theory did not by itself resolve the main problems. It was still necessary to ask how a deterministic theory of social development could be reconciled with the possibility of moral choice (in the context of a single 'natural' or 'phenomenal' world); and further, assuming the reality of moral choice, and the existence of diverse moral ideals, how it was proposed that ethical disagreements should be resolved, and what form of argument would be appropriate, for example, in seeking to show the moral superiority of socialism. Max Adler, as we saw earlier, dealt with some of these questions by assimilating moral impulses and scientific knowledge to the causal process, arguing that they were themselves causal factors amenable to sociological investigation and generalisation. But this view does not meet all the difficulties. It does not make clear whether moral purposes and empirical or theoretical knowledge, which enter into the development of social life as causal agents, are also the products of a causal process, that is to say, merely empirical occurrences, not to be apprehended in terms of their rightness, truth or validity. Furthermore, Adler seems to assume, in a manner very similar to Marx himself, the general progressiveness of social development, and some kind of fortunate coincidence between the factual development of economic and political life and the attainment of a morally superior form of society.

On the other hand, the Hegelian Marxists rejected the distinction between fact and value, science and ethics. Social life, they argued, cannot be treated as the object of a science which would describe and analyse it from the outside. In this sphere men are both subject and object; the development of their knowledge about society is a growth of self-consciousness and a movement of liberation. Knowledge and action are here inseparable, and men's cognition of their situation at the same time prescribes how they should act. In its Marxist form this Hegelian conception assumed a distinctive character; the subject was seen as a collective subject, a social class, and the process of increasing self-awareness was regarded as culminating in the class consciousness of the proletariat. But this view, too, fails to meet all the difficulties which arise in the relation between theory and practice. In the first place, it is just as deterministic as the positivist view; only now the inevitable course of historical development is formulated in terms of 'objective mind' rather than in naturalistic terms. Moreover, the grounds upon which this necessity is asserted are less open to argument and criticism than is the case with the positivist conception, for they are constituted by some kind of insight into the logic of history rather than by empirical observations; and it is difficult to see how the disagreements between different interpretations of history can be rigorously debated if the possibility of empirical tests, in some form or other, is wholly excluded. Lastly, it should be noted that the Hegelian conception, by its insistence upon the idea of a culminating point in the growth of knowledge, is apt to assume a particularly dogmatic form. The attainment of 'absolute knowledge' can be asserted at any historical stage, whether by Hegel in his idealisation of the Prussian State or by Lukács in his idealisation of the Russian Revolution, and how is it then to be controverted, except by the kind of criticism, at once scientific and moral, which Marx originally levelled at Hegel's system?

I am not concerned here to examine in depth the problems of Marxist ethical theory,[1] but only to consider how they bear upon Marxist sociology, and in particular how they might influence a Marxist view of the relation between social theory and social practice. It has become increasingly evident, in the controversies that have gone on since the end of the nineteenth century, that

[1] Though this is an important and neglected sphere of Marxist thought. As S. Stojanovic has observed in his valuable study *Between Ideals and Reality* (New York : Oxford University Press, 1973) : 'A Marxist ethics, at least one worthy of Marx's name, has yet to be constructed' (p. 137). He goes on to review, especially in chapter 9, on 'revolutionary teleology and ethics', some of the major questions with which such an ethical theory would have to deal. Lukács had the intention of writing a systematic work on Marxist ethics, but he was unable to finish more than the long introductory section dealing with ontology (see István Mészáros, *Lukács' Concept of Dialectic*, London : The Merlin Press, 1972, pp. 6–7). Some of the most illuminating writing so far on Marxist ethics is to be found in the essays of Leszek Kolakowski, *Marxism and Beyond* (London : Pall Mall Press, 1969), particularly those on 'responsibility and history'.

some of the fundamental propositions of Marxist theory – concerning the development of the working-class movement, its engagement in political action, and the nature of the transition from capitalist to socialist society – need to be subjected to both scientific and ethical criticism. Repeatedly, from the time of Bernstein to the present day, someone has emerged to declare that he is defending the 'revolutionary core' of Marxism against revisionism and reformism; but this is a meaningless declaration unless it is accompanied by a real analysis of the political forces at work in specific forms of modern society (and especially the presence or absence, whether as constituted realities or as historical tendencies, of revolutionary classes), and by an evaluation of the 'progressive' or 'liberating' character of revolutionary movements and régimes.

The idea of revolution, in the thought of Marx and of later Marxists, manifestly provides the focal point for the discussion of theory and practice, of 'practical–critical activity'; hence a Marxist sociology should be particularly concerned with analysing the concept and studying the historical experiences of revolution. Yet in spite of its importance few Marxist thinkers have made any profound critical examination of the processes of revolutionary change in the modern world. Korsch, as we have seen, regarded the idea of revolutionary change, in opposition to evolutionist conceptions, as one of the four basic principles of Marxist sociology, and a similar view is formulated in Gramsci's criticism of Bukharin. But this methodological postulate – to treat the history of human society as proceeding by a series of 'leaps' from one form of social structure to another – remained largely unexamined. Although it was obviously a fruitful principle to guide inquiry and could find justification in actual social history, especially in modern times, the question to which it gave rise – concerning the relationship between evolutionary and revolutionary change, the association between revolution and violence, and the meaning of revolution in the context of democracy – were not thoroughly explored.

Two Marxist thinkers seem to me to have contributed more than others to a serious analysis of revolution : Rosa Luxemburg, in her pamphlet of 1918 on the Russian Revolution, and Otto Bauer, in a number of essays and books published between 1919 and 1936, selections from which have appeared recently in a French edition.[1] Luxemburg's study, as Nettl remarked, 'was not primarily a discussion of detailed policies. It was an examination of the basic propositions of revolution . . . she was applying well-established, systematic conclusions to a new set of facts.'[2] Thus she asserted the close relationship between a socialist revolution and democracy; criticised the Bolsheviks for their dispersion of the Constituent Assembly, the failure to hold elections, the abolition of freedom of the press and of the rights of association and assembly, the growing reliance upon rule by terror; and indicated the danger that the dictatorship of a *class* would be transformed into the dictatorship of a *party* or *clique*. For Rosa Luxemburg revolution signified a popular movement of liberation, not the establishment of an authoritarian régime which would restrict democratic rights in order to maintain revolutionary leaders in power. 'Lenin', she wrote, 'is completely mistaken in the means he employs. Decree, dictatorial force of the factory overseer, draconic penalties, rule by terror, all these things are but palliatives. The only way to rebirth is the school of public life itself, the most unlimited, the broadest democracy and public opinion. It is rule by terror which demoralizes.'

But still Rosa Luxemburg did not inquire deeply enough into these problems, though she might have done so had she lived to experience the subsequent development of Soviet society. Thus she did not consider the question whether a transition to socialism is possible at all unless bourgeois society has already attained an advanced stage of development with high levels of production and consumption, strongly established democratic practices and widespread experience of the exercise of democratic rights, and a widely diffused scientific and humanistic culture, which would provide a reliable foundation for an extension of human freedom.

[1] Rosa Luxemburg, *The Russian Revolution* (English edn ed. Bertram D. Wolfe, Ann Arbor: University of Michigan Press, 1961); Yvon Bourdet (ed.), *Otto Bauer et la révolution* (Paris: Études et Documentation Internationales, 1968). The question of violence, in relation to the Marxist theory of revolution, was discussed later by M. Merleau Ponty, *Humanisme et terreur* (Paris: Gallimard, 1947).

[2] J. P. Nettl, *Rosa Luxemburg* (London: Oxford University Press, 1966) II, 703–4.

She would perhaps have dismissed such ideas as being reformist in the manner of Kautsky, although her concluding comment that the Russian Revolution could only pose the questions, not resolve them, suggests that she did regard the effective establishment of socialism in the world as depending upon the success of socialist revolutions in some of the more advanced capitalist countries. Again, she did not consider how far the use of revolutionary violence might lead, with more or less necessity, to an authoritarian and hierarchical political régime, might prolong itself in a reign of terror, and thus help to create social institutions and attitudes which it would later be very difficult to reform in a more democratic mould.

Otto Bauer also analysed the Russian Revolution[1] which he regarded, however – from the point of view of its economic and social content – as a bourgeois democratic revolution which had been led, because of the particular circumstances that had developed in Russia, by a working-class party. At that time he thought it possible that the Bolshevik party would liberalise its rule, and the bourgeois character of the revolution would then appear more clearly; but even in a bourgeois republic the working class would retain many of its gains and Russia would remain a powerful factor in the development of working-class democracy throughout the world. Bauer's most important contribution to the study of revolution, however, was his theory of the 'slow revolution.'[2] He made a distinction (as Marx had done) between a political revolution and a social revolution; the former may be sudden and violent, but if it is not accompanied by fundamental changes in the relations of production and in social relations it will amount to no more than the replacement of one ruling minority by another. The changes in social relations, beginning in the sphere of production, constitute the social revolution which develops much more slowly; socialist society can only be constructed gradually, over a long period, through radical reforms in many different spheres of social life.

In Bauer's account the social revolution is seen largely as a

[1] Notably in a pamphlet published in 1921; see Bourdet, *Otto Bauer*, pp. 73–84.

[2] In *Der Weg zum Sozialismus* (Vienna : Wiener Volksbuchhandlung, 1919); see Bourdet, *Otto Bauer*, pp. 87–130.

process of social reorganisation which follows a political revolution, a conquest of power by the working class. But it seems to me more realistic and illuminating to conceive of an 'epoch' of social revolution – that is, a relatively long period of social change and conflict in which the institutions of the old form of society gradually break down or are eroded and a new society takes shape – within which there would occur diverse political revolutions, some of them premature and abortive, others successful in bringing about a significant growth of liberty and equality. Such a conception seems to fit quite well the emergence of capitalist society, which was certainly not the consequence of any single, dramatic political revolution (though many of its characteristic features were sharply delineated in the French Revolution), but resulted from a long sequence of economic and social changes, and a series of political struggles all of which assumed specific forms in each particular country. From this perspective we can regard the period from the late nineteenth century to the present day as an 'age of socialist revolution' in which the Russian Revolution, the revolutionary movements in Western Europe after the First World War, the revolutionary régimes which emerged in different parts of the world after the Second World War, and numerous other political struggles and upheavals, represent so many attempts to advance to a new type of society, in the context of a gradual transformation of economic and social relationships, and cultural values.

But such an interpretation is bound to be much more tentative than any historical account of the origins of capitalist society, for we are still living through these changes, and although we can try to grasp the main trends of development I do not think there is any way at all by which we can *know* how the societies of the present day will be modified, or what new forms of society will succeed them.[1] Only if Marxist sociology were conceived in a strong positivist sense, and at the same time we believed that it had successfully formulated some very general causal laws which

[1] For example, many of the political movements and revolutions of the twentieth century can be interpreted as elements in a transition, not from capitalism to socialism, but from agrarian to industrial societies, as is suggested by Barrington Moore, *Social Origins of Dictatorship and Democracy* (Boston : Beacon Press, 1966).

allowed us to predict the future development of society as a whole and in detail,[1] or alternatively, if it were conceived as a philosophy of history which provided a definitive, incontrovertible insight into the final goal of history, could we treat the *possibility* of a transition to socialism as a *necessity*. Neither of these positions seems to me tenable in the light of all the unresolved difficulties in the construction, testing and comparison of sociological theories; and on the other hand, both tend to encourage dogmatic assertion rather than critical inquiry.

A Marxist sociology, like other sociological systems, needs to be developed in a more tentative, self-critical way. Its aim should be to provide fruitful descriptions, establish significant correlations, and formulate, if it can, causal explanations (which are likely in any case to be of limited generality), while recognising the possibility that the free, conscious activity of men may indeed be able to change the laws of social science. This last point seems anyway to be implied in Marxist thought if the distinction between 'pre-history' and 'history' is taken seriously.[2] Conceived in this way the theoretical scheme stands in a different relation to practical life. As I indicated earlier, the relation cannot be seen as the application of a 'correct' theory in order to reach a desired (and predicted) end, but as a developing interplay of social thought and social action, in which thought has to correct itself by inquiring into, and reflecting upon, past action and its consequences, and to remain open to the possibility of genuine novelty in the process of human self-creation.

It should not be supposed, however, that these questions arise only within a Marxist sociology. All sociology – and for that matter all social science – has a more or less intentional, self-conscious and direct bearing upon practical social life, and in fact has developed, in modern societies, out of a conception

[1] As is perhaps claimed by Marx in the passage I quoted earlier (p. 12 above) from the preface to the second edition of *Capital*.

[2] See especially the discussion in Gajo Petrovic, *Marxism in the Mid-Twentieth Century* (Garden City, N.Y.: Doubleday Anchor, 1967) pp. 90–114, which concludes that the basic sense of Marx's thought is the understanding that man '. . . is not an economic animal, but a practical, hence free, universal, creative and self-creative social being'.

61

of the need for a deliberate, conscious, knowledgeable regulation or planning of man's social existence. A particular virtue of Marxist thought is that it focuses attention explicitly and clearly upon this connection between theory and practice; one of its main weaknesses is that it may become so committed to a specific kind of practice, especially when this practice is embodied in the activities of an organised political party, that the theory becomes uncritical and is treated as a body of established truths which must be defended at all costs in order to ensure the continuance of the practice. In considering, then, the value and validity of a Marxist sociology in relation to other sociological systems, we shall need to be concerned not only with its models of social structure and its explanatory or interpretative propositions, but also with how it, and its rivals, conceive and implement their relation with the practical conduct of social life, and more especially with political action.

5. SOCIOLOGY : MARXIST AND OTHER

There are numerous reasons for approaching with great caution, and even scepticism, an attempt to portray Marxism as a distinctive system of sociology. First, as the earlier discussion should have made clear, Marxism itself is far from being a homogeneous or unified body of thought. The controversies which have taken place during the past hundred years have produced very diverse interpretations and even 'schools' of Marxist thought. There is a major division between those who conceive of Marxism as a philosophical world view, or a philosophy of history, and those who conceive of it primarily as a general social science, or sociology; but there are still many differences of opinion within each of these broad conceptions – about the basic ideas of the Marxist system, about the interpretation of particular forms of society or historical events, and about the relation of a Marxist analysis to the choice of political action in any given set of circumstances.

In terms of the conception of Marxism as a world view the place of sociology is very uncertain. It might be denied altogether that there is any need for a general social science, or its role might be restricted, as by Gramsci, to the carrying out of social surveys (that is, to what might be better called 'social statistics'). On the other hand, a distinctive theory of society might be conceived as being strictly dependent upon the world view – upon its ontology, theory of knowledge, and ethics – so that one could define a 'Marxist sociology' in the same way as a 'Christian sociology', a 'Hindu sociology', or perhaps a 'humanist sociology' might be defined. But this does not seem a very plausible or fruitful idea – and it has certainly not been worked out very fully in Marxist thought – for although every sociological theory raises philosophical questions, which need to be considered from the standpoint of the philosophy of science and also of the sociology of knowledge, it is not the case at all that the construction and development of sociological theories has depended upon, or does depend upon, the prior elaboration of, and continual reference to, a total world view.

However, if we then adopt the other principal conception and treat Marxism as being primarily a sociological system, further difficulties confront us, since sociology too is far from being a homogeneous and unified body of thought. From the beginning, in spite of the existence of common themes and problems, there have been very diverse 'schools', numerous 'unsettled questions', and apparently incommensurable theories; and in recent years the proliferation of doctrines and points of view has reached a stage which some see as a challenging intellectual crisis, others (more gloomily) as a state of almost total incoherence. In order to define the specific characteristics of a Marxist sociology, and especially to judge its validity and fruitfulness in relation to other types of sociology, we need a more or less stable broader framework of conceptions defining what is to count as a 'good' sociological theory, an 'adequate' method, and 'acceptable' criteria for testing or judging propositions. All this, however, is in dispute, and what seems to be happening is that various strange alliances of Marxist and non-Marxist thought emerge which propound one or other notion – positivist, phenomenological, and so on – of the logic of sociology.

Finally, there is a third difficulty, partly connected with what I have just said, in specifying a distinctive Marxist sociology. It is obvious that some versions of Marxism at any rate have been greatly influenced by, and have incorporated ideas from, other styles of social thought; for example, phenomenology, existentialism and structuralism. Still more important in the present case is the fact that sociological thought has incorporated, though often in modified ways, many Marxist conceptions – for example, of class, social conflict, ideology – and that some of the most significant controversies in sociology have revolved around ideas and theories which have their source in Marx's thought. To some extent, therefore, we can agree that a process of assimilation has been taking place along the lines that Kolakowski has sketched: '. . . with the gradual refinement of research techniques in the humanities, the concept of Marxism as a separate school of

66

thought will in time become blurred and ultimately disappear altogether. . . . What is permanent in Marx's work will be assimilated in the natural course of scientific development.'[1] Of course, many different outcomes are still possible. Sociology might become more Marxist if a large number of Marx's basic propositions could be strongly established against the criticisms that have been formulated; or on the other hand a large part of Marx's work might be so radically revised, or discarded altogether, as a result of new discoveries that only a vestige of its distinctive notions remained in the general body of sociological thought.

Taking into account these various difficulties I shall try to set out what seems to me still distinctive and valuable in Marxism as sociology, while recognising that my argument will depend upon a particular conception of the domain and purpose of both sociology and Marxism which I cannot elaborate here : of sociology as an empirical science which comprises observation statements of diverse kinds within a theoretical framework, and aims to establish classifications of social phenomena, functional correlations and causal or quasi-causal[2] connections; of Marxism as an attempt to construct and develop a general social science in this sense.

A useful starting-point for this discussion is Karl Korsch's sketch of the principles of a Marxist sociology (see above, p. 39). Leaving aside the question of *praxis*, which I examined in the previous chapter, there are four main points in Korsch's account. First, the primacy of the economic structure in the Marxist analysis of society, which Korsch expresses by saying that Marxism could be regarded as *political economy* rather than *sociology*; second, the historical location or specification of all social phenomena; third, the setting of empirical studies of particular social phenomena within a historical economic context; and fourth, the

[1] Leszek Kolakowski, *Marxism and Beyond* (London : Pall Mall Press, 1969) p. 204.
[2] By 'quasi-causal' I mean a type of causal relation in which the connection between cause and effect is mediated by consciousness; see the discussion in G. H. von Wright, *Explanation and Understanding* (London : Routledge & Kegan Paul, 1971) chapter IV. This also has a bearing upon problems concerning the nature of the observations that can be made in sociological research.

recognition of revolutionary as well as evolutionary social changes, of the occurrence of breaks in historical continuity in the transition from one form of society to another.

As to the first point, it does undoubtedly indicate one of the principal distinguishing features of Marxist social theory. It is not simply that a great deal of modern sociology has ignored the economic structure, or has assigned it a minor place, in analysing a total social system (so that sociology frequently appeared to be a science of the non-economic aspects of social life); but that no other sociological theory has made the 'mode of production of material life' one of its fundamental categories. As I have described this difference elsewhere :

> Unlike other sociological systems that treat society as an autonomous subject and take its existence in the natural world as something given, Marx's theory is based firmly upon the idea of a relationship between society and nature. Its fundamental concept is 'human labour', viewed in a historical perspective; it is the developing interchange between man and nature, which at the same time creates, and progressively transforms, social relationships among men.[1]

But this basic idea has attracted criticism both within and outside Marxist thought, and the question of the relation between the economic 'base' and the social and cultural 'superstructure' has presented notorious difficulties of interpretation. It is not easy to formulate, either in a general way or in particular cases, the precise 'determining' force of economic changes, as against other diverse social influences; or, if the primacy of the economy is strongly emphasised, to avoid arriving at a 'technological' interpretation of history.

Many sociological critics of Marxism have drawn attention to the importance of non-economic factors in social development, the best-known general criticism being Max Weber's account of the role of the Protestant ethic in the development of Western capitalism, and his depiction of an overall process of 'rationalisation' of social life, which was intended to complement and modify

[1] T. B. Bottomore (ed.), *Karl Marx* (Englewood Cliffs, N.J. : Prentice-Hall, 1973) pp. 38–9.

the Marxist theory. More recently, Talcott Parsons has taken a more extreme view, substituting a 'spiritualist' for a 'materialistic' interpretation of history : 'I believe that, within the social system, the normative elements are more important for social change than the "material interests" of constitutive units.'[1] However, this is an affirmation of faith, not a demonstration. It is evident, none the less, that many non-economic forces in social life, which are more or less autonomous though they may sometimes be connected with economic interests – the growth of science, nationalism, political democracy, religious beliefs and religious communities, ethnic groups – have a significant influence upon social change and the occurrence of social conflict. Such forces have often been neglected by Marxist thinkers, and even where they have been taken into account it has usually proved difficult to assimilate them into the main scheme of interpretation in terms of the development of a mode of production and class relations.[2]

But a still more radical criticism of the very basis of Marx's theory, the concept of human labour, has been formulated within Marxist thought itself in the work of the later Frankfurt School.[3] It is directed against that strand in Marx's thought which interprets the historical development of human society solely in terms of a process of labour conceived as the production of material objects; and it opposes to this conception a view of human nature and human self-creation based upon two characteristics of man, as a tool-maker and a language-user. Thus, Habermas distinguishes two aspects of human activity – 'labour' and 'interaction', or 'instrumental behaviour' and 'communicative

[1] Talcott Parsons, *Societies: Evolutionary and Comparative Perspectives* (Englewood Cliffs, N.J. : Prentice-Hall, 1966) p. 113.

[2] The Austro-Marxists contributed more than other Marxist writers to an analysis of nationality and nationalism, since they had to face these questions in political life in the old Austro-Hungarian Empire. See especially Otto Bauer, *Die Nationalitätenfrage und die Sozialdemokratie* (Vienna : Marx-Studien, 2, 1907).

[3] See especially, Jürgen Habermas, *Knowledge and Human Interests* (London : Heinemann, 1972), and the general discussion of this question in Albrecht Wellmer, *Critical Theory of Society*, chapter 2. Some of the ideas on which this later criticism is based were originally formulated in the 1930s by Max Horkheimer; see his essays collected in *Kritische Theorie* (Frankfurt : S. Fischer, 1968).

behaviour'. Of course, these ideas derive to a large extent from Marx's own work, since he often used the term 'labour' in a very broad sense (especially in his early writings), so that it could be taken as roughly equivalent to human activity or the exercise of human creative powers in general, whether in the development of material production, in the edification of social institutions, or in the creation of cultural objects. But still it is the case that Marx's historical and sociological theory gave a crucial importance to the development of the forms of material labour and production, and to the class struggles arising directly from 'economic contradictions'. The criticisms of this conception elaborated by the Frankfurt School reintroduce elements of German idealist philosophy (in the shape of the activity of abstract reason), as well as an indeterminacy in the interpretation of social events, because they remove from its privileged position the single, powerful engine of discovery and explanation that Marx provided in his economic interpretation. The distinctiveness of Marxist sociology becomes obscured in a new philosophy of history which gives a stronger emphasis to the role of 'spiritual' factors in social development, but at the same time is less able to define clearly the forces at work in social struggles or the main trends of change.

The second distinguishing feature of Marxist sociology, according to Korsch, is its principle of 'historical specification'. This does not separate Marxism quite so sharply from other kinds of sociology, since many of them — the 'social evolutionism' of the nineteenth century, Max Weber's historical sociology — also attempt to relate particular social phenomena to the general characteristics of an epoch or a type of society. It is rather the content of the Marxist historical scheme — its classification of societies in terms of their mode of production and the point they have reached in a sequence which Marx described as 'progressive epochs in the economic formation of society' — that marks a difference. But this aspect of the Marxist theory has also been subjected to much criticism, again from within Marxism as well as from outside. First, there are the well-known difficulties of locating in the Marxist scheme the form of society that Marx called 'Asiatic'.[1] Further, it seems to be the case that two of the

[1] See the essay by George Lichtheim, 'Marx and the "Asiatic Mode of Production"', reprinted in his book *The Concept of*

70

types of society that Marx distinguished, the feudal and the modern capitalist, have been much more amenable to a Marxist analysis, and they have certainly been more thoroughly studied, whereas Marxist studies of the earlier form of society that Marx called 'primitive communism' have so far been less common and less fruitful.[1]

However there have also been more fundamental criticisms of the whole Marxist historical approach, issuing mainly from the new 'structuralist' school of thought.[2] The nature of these criticisms may be illustrated briefly from the work of Claude Lévi-Strauss, whose intention seems to be to uncover the basic and universal structural elements of all human societies. As he writes in the concluding chapter of *The Savage Mind*, in his controversy with Sartre : 'Ethnographic analysis tries to arrive at invariants beyond the empirical diversity of human societies. . . .' This is not unlike the outlook of the earlier structural–functionalist school of sociology which was preoccupied with the search for universal 'functional prerequisites' of society; the main difference seems

---

Ideology and Other Essays (New York : Random House, 1967); and also the general discussion of Marx's historical scheme by Eric Hobsbawm in his introduction to Karl Marx, *Pre-Capitalist Economic Formations* (London : Lawrence & Wishart, 1964).

[1] See, for a general account of Marxism and social anthropology, Raymond Firth, *The Sceptical Anthropologist? Social Anthropology and Marxist Views on Society*, Proceedings of the British Academy, vol. LVIII (London, 1972). Marx himself had a strong interest in the earlier forms of society, and he devoted much time in the last few years of his life to studies in this field. His notebooks from that period have recently been published with an extensive commentary by L. Krader (ed.), *The Ethnological Notebooks of Karl Marx* (Assen : Van Gorcum, 1972), and they provide useful material for a reassessment of the Marxist conception of early societies. There is, as Firth notes, a considerable revival of interest at the present time in a more critical Marxist anthropology, particularly in relation to colonialism and to peasant societies.

[2] The main ideas of structuralism are presented and criticised in David Robey (ed.), *Structuralism: An Introduction* (Oxford : University Press, 1973), and in W. G. Runciman, *Sociology in its Place* (Cambridge : University Press, 1970) chapter 2, 'What Is Structuralism?'

to lie in Lévi-Strauss's claim that he is concerned with deeper levels of structure, and in his desire to connect the structural elements of society with the structure of the human mind and eventually with the structure of the brain (hence the reductionism of his method). His approach is intentionally anti-historical – 'it is vain to go to historical consciousness for the truest meaning' – and establishes history and anthropology (or sociology) as complementary in the particular sense that there could not, and should not, be an historical anthropology or sociology. But although the structuralist type of inquiry produces some interesting material (above all in linguistics and in a more limited way in anthropology) its contribution to sociology has not so far been significant; and it seems to evade the most important questions, which are precisely those of the determinants of diverse forms of social structure and the historical passage from one to another.

An outpost of structuralism has been established in Marxist territory in the shape of Althusser's version of Marxism.[1] I cannot examine here this particularly obscure body of thought,[2] but the manner of approaching the relation between 'structure' and 'history' is illustrated in an essay by Maurice Godelier.[3] After a somewhat trivial argument intended to show that Marx was a structuralist *avant la lettre* Godelier propounds as one of his main themes the pre-eminence of structural over historical analysis : 'The genesis of a structure can only be studied under the "guidance" of a pre-existing knowledge of that structure.' But the converse is equally true in the case of a Marxist analysis; the structure of a particular social formation (for example, capitalism) can only be studied on the basis of a pre-established historical scheme which gives a preliminary definition of its characteristics and location in a sequence. Marxist sociology always involves both historical and structural analysis and a con-

[1] See especially, Louis Althusser and Étienne Balibar, *Reading Capital* (London : New Left Books, 1970).
[2] Its pretensions are brilliantly demolished in an essay by L. Kolakowski, 'Althusser's Marx', *The Socialist Register* (London : The Merlin Press, 1971) pp. 111–28.
[3] Maurice Godelier, 'System, Structure and Contradiction in *Capital*', *The Socialist Register* (London : The Merlin Press, 1967) pp. 91–119.

tinual movement between these two modes.

The structuralist approach also involves another kind of narrowing of the Marxist conception. It seems to be claimed that once the basic structure of a social formation has been uncovered the phenomena of genesis and transformation are to be treated as features of this abstract structure itself. The historical process is then reduced to a 'ghostly dance of bloodless categories', and the interaction between a given structure on one side and the conscious activities of real-life individuals and social groups on the other – which has a major importance in Marx's own accounts of social change – is eliminated from the scheme of explanation. It need only be added here that the structuralist analyses have not yet produced any specially illuminating interpretations of the principal trends in the development of twentieth-century capitalist societies.

The third issue raised by Korsch can be dealt with more briefly. As I pointed out earlier, Marxist sociology has largely failed to develop empirical studies of particular social phenomena. There have not been significant and extensive Marxist contributions to the study of crime and delinquency, bureaucracy, political parties, the family, or to a great number of other specialised fields of inquiry; and even in the study of social class and stratification – which occupies a crucial place in the Marxist theory – there is a notable absence of the thorough historical and sociological investigations that might have been expected. More generally it might be said that Marxist sociology has not had the innovating role, in opening up new fields of research and advancing new theses, that should have emerged, in the course of its scientific development, from the originality of its initial formulations. In recent years, however, there have been signs of a much greater impact of Marxist thought upon sociological research, and of a more adequate elaboration of Marxist theory based upon research. One example, with which I happen to be especially familiar, is the influence of critical studies inspired by Marxism, though often revising or adding to some traditional Marxist conceptions, of the 'developing countries' and the whole process of development and underdevelopment. These studies, beginning with Paul Baran's *The Political Economy of Growth*[1] and con-

[1] (New York : Monthly Review Press, 1962.)

tinuing in the work of A. G. Frank and others,[1] have brought about a radical reformulation of the questions posed in the study of development and have revived, in a new context, Marxist analyses of the global economic and social system of capitalism and of the complex relationships of imperialism and dependence.

The last differentiating feature that Korsch suggests is the concern of Marxist sociology with processes of revolutionary change. This does quite clearly separate Marxism from those sociological theories which either pay little attention to social change and concentrate upon the enduring, timeless or cyclical aspects of social life, or else conceive change as a gradual, evolutionary process of increasing social differentiation or the cumulative advance of knowledge, and so on (in the manner of Spencer and Parsons). There are, in fact, two ideas involved in the Marxist theory: one is that of breaks in historical continuity, of massive transitions to a new form of society; the other, that of social change through conflict between antagonistic groups. In our own century of revolution these elements of Marxist sociology must necessarily appear more realistic, more likely to lead to a genuine understanding of social development, than the ideas of the rival sociological theories. But still there are many unresolved problems, some of which I have considered in the previous chapter. The relation between evolutionary and revolutionary changes needs to be more thoroughly explored, the nature of revolutionary epochs has to be characterised in a more precise way, and the problems posed by the development of the working-class movement in capitalist societies in non-revolutionary forms, which may lead to evolutionist formulations of the Marxist theory itself (as by Bernstein), have to be more carefully examined. Again, in this particular context Marxist thought can be criticised for having failed to stimulate the empirical studies, or the reflections based upon empirical investigations, that would have advanced the theory of revolutionary change beyond its expression as a very abstract principle or model.

[1] A. G. Frank, *Capitalism and Underdevelopment in Latin America*, 2nd edn (New York: Monthly Review Press, 1969). See also the selected readings in Henry Bernstein (ed.), *Underdevelopment and Development* (Harmondsworth: Penguin, 1973).

*   *   *   *   *

In the foregoing discussion I have tried to elicit the principal features of a Marxist sociology conceived as an empirical science, and at the same time to indicate some of its strengths and weaknesses. It should be borne in mind, when considering the extent of the criticism which it has attracted, that other sociological theories have been exposed to even more damaging criticism; and that no other general theory has shown anything like the same power to define and analyse significant problems in the development of societies, to formulate quasi-causal connections, and to provoke argument on fundamental theoretical issues. But still it may be said that Marxist sociology – though again like some other theories – is too bold in its claims to understand and explain social life; that it has not been prepared to recognise the limitations of *all* sociological thought faced with the vast complexity of social interaction and the human potentiality for creative innovation. This boldness, tending toward dogmatism, is evidently connected with another distinctive feature of Marxism, namely its commitment to the ideal of socialism as a future form of society. Here again, however, it only displays in a more pronounced manner one of the characteristics of sociology as a 'moral science' which, as Durkheim claimed, naturally prolongs itself in philosophical reflection, and indeed often has its starting-point there. What is important is to maintain a certain distance between the sociology and the philosophy, and to conceive the sociological domain clearly as one where rival theories contend in their explanations of the facts of social life. The idea of socialism as a possible and desirable future helps to guide Marxist sociology in its choice of significant problems, in the conduct of worthwhile research, and in the criticism of rival interpretations; but the idea of the inevitability of socialism – its inscription among the facts of social life – has tended to impoverish and deform Marxist thought.

BIBLIOGRAPHY

I. General Studies

Max Adler, *Der soziologische Sinn der Lehre von Karl Marx* (Leipzig: C. L. Hirschfeld, 1914). Formulates the principles of Marxism as a system of sociology in terms of the basic concept of 'socialised mankind'.

S. Avineri, *The Social and Political Theory of Karl Marx* (Cambridge: Cambridge University Press, 1968). Provides an excellent analysis of some of the fundamental concepts of Marx's sociology.

Norman Birnbaum, *Toward a Critical Sociology* (New York: Oxford University Press, 1971) pp. 94–129, 'The Crisis of Marxist Sociology'. Examines the problems posed for Marxist theory by recent social changes.

T. B. Bottomore and M. Rubel (eds), *Karl Marx: Selected Writings in Sociology and Social Philosophy* (Harmondsworth: Penguin Books, 1963). The introduction reviews some aspects of the development of Marxism and sociology.

Benedetto Croce, *Historical Materialism and the Economics of Karl Marx*, translated by C. M. Meredith, with an introduction by A. D. Lindsay (London: Howard Latimer, 1913). Discusses in several chapters the sociological and philosophical significance of 'historical materialism'.

Georges Gurvitch, *La Vocation actuelle de la sociologie*, rev. edn, 2 vols (Paris: Presses Universitaires de France, 1963) chapter 12, 'La Sociologie de Karl Marx'. An expanded version of an essay which gave particular attention to the sociological ideas in Marx's early writings, in relation to Saint-Simon, and which now analyses the whole of Marx's work from a sociological perspective.

Karl Korsch, *Karl Marx* (London: Chapman & Hall, 1938).

Published in a series on 'Modern Sociologists' Korsch's study examines three main aspects of Marx's work: the analysis of modern bourgeois society, political economy and the theory of history.

Henri Lefebvre, *The Sociology of Marx* (New York: Pantheon Books, 1968). A rather abstract philosophical discussion of the sociological elements in Marx's thought.

G. Lichtheim, *From Marx to Hegel and Other Essays* (London: Orbach & Chambers, 1971). Several essays in this volume provide a good account of recent tendencies in Marxist social thought and consider some aspects of the relation between Marxism and sociology.

Karl Löwith, 'Max Weber und Karl Marx', *Archiv für Sozialwissenschaft und Sozialpolitik*, LXVI (1932) part 1, pp. 53–99, and part 2, pp. 175–214. An illuminating comparison between the general sociological orientations of Weber and Marx. An English translation is due to appear shortly.

J. A. Schumpeter, *Capitalism, Socialism and Democracy* (New York: Harper & Row, 1942) chapter II, 'Marx the Sociologist'. A short, critical account of Marxism as an empirical science, concentrating on the relation between the economic system and the social superstructure.

II. *Studies in Particular Areas of Sociology*

Norman Birnbaum, 'Conflicting Interpretations of the Rise of Capitalism: Marx and Weber', *British Journal of Sociology*, IV (1953) 125–41.

A. Giddens, 'Marx, Weber and the Development of Capitalism', *Sociology*, IV (1970) 289–310.

Lucien Goldman, *Marxisme et sciences humaines* (Paris: Gallimard, 1970). A number of essays in this volume discuss and exemplify the use of Marxist conceptions in the study of culture.

G. Lichtheim, 'Marx and the "Asiatic Mode of Production"', *St Antony's Papers*, no. 14 (London: Chatto & Windus, 1963).

G. Lukács, *History and Class Consciousness* (London: The Merlin Press, 1971). Lukács's Hegelian presentation of the Marxist theory of class is discussed critically in some of the essays in István Mészáros (ed.), *Aspects of History and Class Consciousness* (London : Routledge & Kegan Paul, 1971).

S. Ossowski, *Class Structure in the Social Consciousness* (London : Routledge & Kegan Paul, 1963) chapter 5, 'The Marxian Synthesis'. A good critical account of the various elements that entered into Marx's concept of class.